© Stonewell Healing Press, 2025
All rights reserved.

This book is a labor of care. Please do not copy, share, or distribute any part of it—digitally or physically—without written permission from the author or publisher, except for brief excerpts used in reviews or critical articles. Your respect helps this work reach others who need it.

This workbook is not a replacement for therapy, crisis support, or mental health treatment. It's meant to offer reflection, comfort, and growth—not clinical care. If you're struggling, please reach out to a licensed professional. You matter too much to go through it alone.

Every effort has been made to ensure this content is accurate, responsible, and thoughtful. The author and publisher cannot guarantee outcomes and are not liable for misuse or misinterpretation of the material.

Thank you for being here. We're honored to walk beside you.

M. Tourangeau
Stonewell Healing Press

TABLE OF CONTENTS

SECTION 1 -   **12**

Understanding Grief & Complex Emotions After Abortion

SECTION 2-   **40**

The Unspoken Weight of Guilt and Shame

SECTION 3 -   **64**

Reclaiming Your Power and Autonomy

SECTION 4 -   **88**

Finding Peace with the Past

SECTION 5-   **114**

Reclaiming Your Power

SECTION 6   **134**

Embracing Your Healing Journey

Stonewell Healing Press

TABLE OF CONTENTS

SECTION 7 -   154
Healing Through Connection

SECTION 8-   180
Forgiveness—Releasing the Burden of Guilt

SECTION 9 -   198
Reclaiming Your Power—Embracing the Path Forward

SECTION 10 -   222
Embracing Peace - Living With Yourself After the Journey

SECTION 11 -   240
The Future, Reimagined - Navigating the Emotions of Future Pregnancies

---

CLOSING   260

Stonewell Healing Press

Dedicated to those who had to
break their own heart.

STONEWELL HEALING PRESS

HOW TO USE THIS WORKBOOK

Take your time with this. The more you pause to really think about each question and answer honestly, the more space you create for reflection. And with deeper reflection, this experience can open up new understanding and healing you might not expect.

Be honest with yourself—there's no judgment here. This is your private space. If you want, you can even throw this book away or burn it later to keep your secrets safe. That said, be mindful of how much you dive in. Healing and reflection around tough, sensitive topics can bring up strong feelings—and yes, it can get triggering. So here's your gentle trigger warning.

The real progress comes when you practice the skills, not just read about them. The more you try them out in your life, the more helpful this workbook will be.

STONEWELL HEALING PRESS

ASSESSMENT

WHERE AM I NOW?

Before we begin, take a moment to honestly check in with yourself by rating these statements on a scale from 1 (not at all) to 10 (completely):

1-10

1. I feel able to acknowledge and honor all of my emotions—even the conflicting or uncomfortable ones—without self-judgment.

2. I feel genuine compassion and forgiveness toward myself for the choices I've made and the experiences I've lived.

3. I feel confident in my ability to make decisions that reflect my values, needs, and boundaries.

4. I feel clarity and understanding about the ways my past experiences impact my emotions and relationships today.

5. I feel capable of holding hope for the future while allowing myself to fully feel past grief and loss.

6. I feel supported and understood by people, communities, or practices that honor my experience.

7. I feel able to navigate conversations, social expectations, or judgments about my experience without losing my emotional center.

8. I feel empowered to reclaim my personal strength, autonomy, and agency in my healing journey and in life moving forward.

SECTION ONE

Understanding Grief & Complex Emotions After Abortion

Grief after an abortion is unique. Unlike the more publicly acknowledged forms of loss, abortion grief can feel complicated and hidden. You might grieve the life you didn't live, the dreams you didn't have the chance to see unfold, or the silence around your experience. It can feel isolating, especially when the world often moves on or minimizes your pain.

This section is about understanding that grief is more than just sadness. It's a complex, multifaceted experience that can bring up a range of emotions: guilt, shame, relief, confusion, anger, and even peace. It's important to acknowledge that all of these emotions are valid, even if they feel contradictory at times. They are part of your story. Here, we'll explore the different facets of grief, from emotional and cognitive responses to physical and somatic manifestations. We'll also talk about how grief can show up in unexpected ways, including how it can impact your self-identity and relationships. By the end of this section, you'll have a better understanding of what you're feeling and why, which will help you move toward healing with greater compassion for yourself.

Making Sense Of It
The Complexity of Abortion Grief

Grief after abortion rarely fits into neat boxes. It doesn't follow the tidy timelines we're taught to expect, and it doesn't always look like the grief the world recognizes. Instead, it shows up in flashes: a pang of sadness when you see a pregnancy announcement, a deep exhale of relief that life could move forward, an ache that has no words, or even anger at the silence surrounding your pain. Sometimes all these feelings live inside the same breath. That contradiction can feel disorienting, but it doesn't mean you're broken — it means you've lived through something layered, something deeply human.

Part of what makes abortion grief so complex is the lack of permission to grieve openly. When a child dies, there are rituals, condolences, and social scripts that tell you how to mourn. After abortion, most people receive none of that. There is no funeral, no memorial, no socially sanctioned ritual for closure. Instead, grief often takes place in isolation, tucked away in private moments when the world isn't looking. This silence doesn't just make the grief harder — it can make you question whether your pain is even valid. Yet grief doesn't need permission to exist. It simply does.

And then there's the cultural weight. In many societies, womanhood — or personhood in relation to reproduction — is tied to motherhood, selflessness, and sacrifice. Against that backdrop, abortion can feel like a transgression, even if you stand firmly by your decision. Messages from family, media, or religion may whisper (or scream) that you've broken an unspoken contract.

Making Sense Of It
The Complexity of Abortion Grief

Even if those voices aren't yours, they can burrow deep, creating guilt or shame that isn't truly yours to carry. Grief, then, isn't only about the pregnancy itself — it's about navigating a world that has already written a story about you without your consent.

Relationships add another layer. Some people carry grief alone because their partner won't or can't talk about it. Others feel pressure to stay silent for fear of judgment. And still others wrestle with unspoken resentments — "Why wasn't I supported more?" or "Why didn't anyone see how hard this was for me?" — that deepen the ache. Isolation doesn't just come from culture at large; it can also live inside the walls of your closest relationships.

The body, too, carries its own story. Even after your mind makes peace with your choice, your body may hold sensations that resurface unexpectedly — tension in your chest, a stomach that knots during anniversaries, a heaviness that arrives before you even realize why. Relief and grief can live side by side in your nervous system. The body doesn't measure morality; it remembers experience. And sometimes, the body grieves what the mind can't yet name.

It's also important to remember that grief after abortion doesn't always show up as sorrow. For some, it's a fierce wave of relief, even gratitude. For others, it's numbness, as though the emotions are too large to touch all at once.

Making Sense Of It
The Complexity of Abortion Grief

Some people feel sadness for what could have been, while others feel grief for who they were before the choice. Some carry all of this at once, layered and shifting over time. None of these responses are wrong. They're all threads in the fabric of your lived experience.

What matters most is this: your grief, however it shows up, belongs. You don't have to justify it. You don't have to make it neat. It doesn't have to look like anyone else's. Healing isn't about choosing between guilt or peace, sorrow or relief. It's about giving each of those truths a seat at the table of your life. When you allow grief to be as complex as it really is — not simplified, not silenced — you give yourself the chance to move forward with honesty, compassion, and dignity.

What emotions am I experiencing right now that I might not have fully acknowledged?

Take a deep breath and allow yourself to notice what comes up in your body and mind. Are there feelings you've been avoiding or pushing away? Grief often carries emotions we don't expect, like relief, anger, or numbness. Write them down, and allow yourself to feel them without judgment. Your feelings are part of your journey.

What emotions am I experiencing right now that I might not have fully acknowledged?

What emotions am I experiencing right now that I might not have fully acknowledged?

Take a deep breath and allow yourself to notice what comes up in your body and mind. Are there feelings you've been avoiding or pushing away? Grief often carries emotions we don't expect, like relief, anger, or numbness. Write them down, and allow yourself to feel them without judgment. Your feelings are part of your journey.

What emotions am I experiencing right now that I might not have fully acknowledged?

What emotions am I experiencing right now that I might not have fully acknowledged?

Take a deep breath and allow yourself to notice what comes up in your body and mind. Are there feelings you've been avoiding or pushing away? Grief often carries emotions we don't expect, like relief, anger, or numbness. Write them down, and allow yourself to feel them without judgment. Your feelings are part of your journey.

What emotions am I experiencing right now that I might not have fully acknowledged?

What emotions am I experiencing right now that I might not have fully acknowledged?

Take a deep breath and allow yourself to notice what comes up in your body and mind. Are there feelings you've been avoiding or pushing away? Grief often carries emotions we don't expect, like relief, anger, or numbness. Write them down, and allow yourself to feel them without judgment. Your feelings are part of your journey.

What emotions am I experiencing right now that I might not have fully acknowledged?

What emotions am I experiencing right now that I might not have fully acknowledged?

Take a deep breath and allow yourself to notice what comes up in your body and mind. Are there feelings you've been avoiding or pushing away? Grief often carries emotions we don't expect, like relief, anger, or numbness. Write them down, and allow yourself to feel them without judgment. Your feelings are part of your journey.

What emotions am I experiencing right now that I might not have fully acknowledged?

TRACING THE TRUTH

GIVING SHAPE TO THE SILENCE

Because abortion grief is often hidden, many carry it in silence. This exercise offers you a safe way to bring voice to what has been unspoken — without needing anyone else's validation.

Why it helps:
By externalizing grief, you remove the burden of carrying it silently inside your body. This creative dialogue allows you to acknowledge grief as real, but not as your entire identity. It makes the invisible visible — which is the first step toward relief, clarity, and eventual healing.

Imagine your grief as an object. What shape, weight, texture, or color does it have?
Write a one-page "letter" from that object to you. What would it say if it could speak?
Now, write a letter back — what do you want to say to this grief that has lived inside you?

TRACING THE TRUTH

GIVING SHAPE TO THE SILENCE

TRACING THE TRUTH

GIVING SHAPE TO THE SILENCE

TRACING THE TRUTH

GIVING SHAPE TO THE SILENCE

TRACING THE TRUTH

NAMING THE CONTRADICTIONS

After abortion, emotions rarely line up neatly. You may feel sadness and relief in the same breath, or guilt alongside gratitude. This exercise helps you hold those contradictions without forcing yourself to "pick a side."

Why it helps:
This practice makes space for emotional paradox — grief that is both pain and relief, sorrow and peace. Instead of seeing conflicting emotions as proof of "confusion" or "wrongness," it allows you to see them as layers of a whole truth. That shift can reduce shame and help you feel more integrated.

On one page, write the sentence: "One truth I feel is…" and finish it honestly.
On the opposite page, write: "Another truth I also feel is…" and finish it. Keep going, alternating, until you've written down 6–10 truths that might feel opposite or overlapping.
When finished, read them back slowly. Notice how they can coexist without cancelling each other out.

TRACING THE TRUTH

NAMING THE CONTRADICTIONS

TRACING THE TRUTH

NAMING THE CONTRADICTIONS

TRACING THE TRUTH

NAMING THE CONTRADICTIONS

EXTERNALIZE THE INNER CRITIC

The inner critic often masquerades as truth, when really it's a protective part gone overboard. By externalizing it — drawing it, collaging it, or writing it as a character — you create distance. Suddenly, it's not you failing; it's a scared or rigid part doing its job too harshly. Research in IFS and narrative therapy shows that putting dialogue on paper softens shame and restores self-leadership. Adding a Wise Friend voice gives you access to compassion and balance. The final boundary statement reminds the critic: its role is protection, not punishment. That's where healing starts.

Create the Critic — Draw, doodle, or collage how your inner critic might look. Don't worry about artistic skill.

Dialogue — Write a short back-and-forth:
You: "I hear you saying I'll fail."
Critic: "I don't want you to get hurt."
Wise Friend: "You can protect without tearing down."

Set a Boundary — End the dialogue with a firm line: "Your job is protection, not punishment. I'll take it from here."

MAPPING YOUR RESILIENCE

When life is painful, the spotlight lands on what's broken or lost. But every hard season you've lived through also carries evidence of your resilience. Mapping your past with a "strength lens" helps you reclaim those forgotten skills — endurance, creativity, boundary-setting, persistence, humor, or compassion. Trauma research shows that naming and revisiting these strengths rebuilds self-trust. Instead of seeing your past only as a string of wounds, you begin to recognize the ways you showed up for yourself. Circling three core strengths creates a personal toolkit you can consciously bring forward into your next chapter.

1 **Draw Your Timeline** —Mark a few "hard seasons" you've lived through on the timeline.

2 **Name Strengths** — Under each event, write one or two strengths you used to get through (e.g., courage, asking for help, persistence).

3 **Circle Three** — Look at the whole map. Circle three strengths that feel most alive, relevant, or needed for where you're headed now.

4 **Carry Them Forward** — Write them on a sticky note or card where you'll see them often — reminders that you've done hard things before, and you will again.

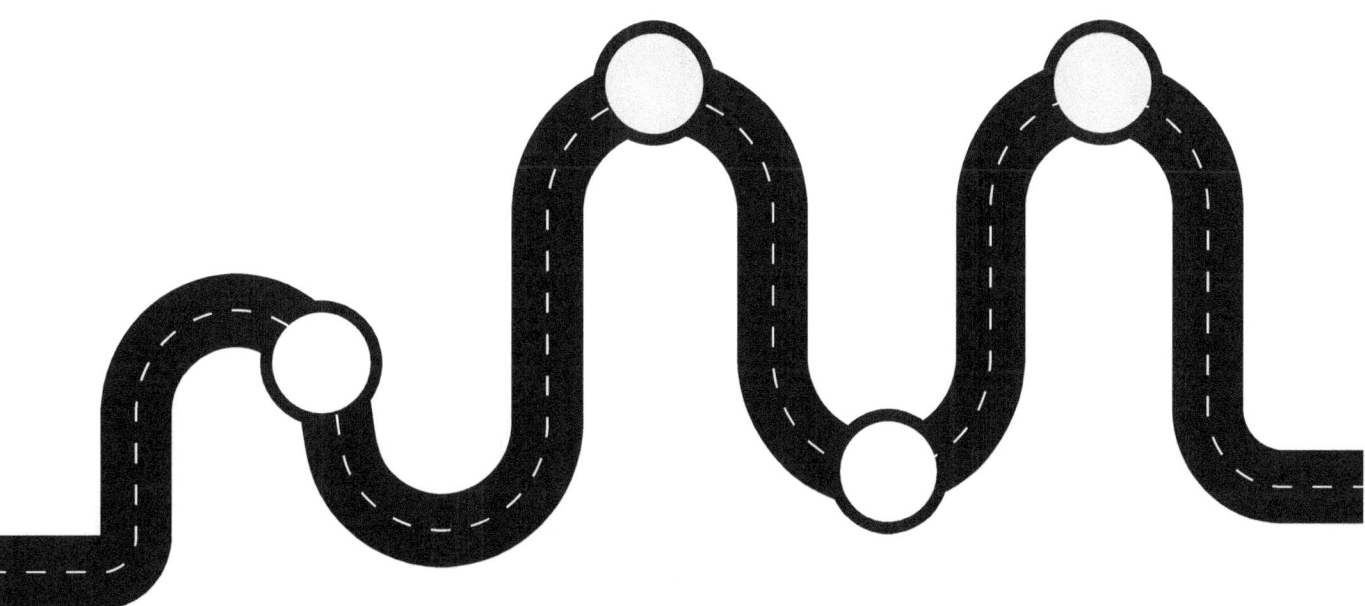

SAFE/BRAVE COLLAGE

Healing doesn't mean throwing yourself into the deep end. It means finding the edges of your current safety and gently stretching them. This exercise blends comfort and courage, showing your nervous system that bravery doesn't have to mean danger. Visual imagery (like collage) activates deeper parts of the brain than words alone, helping you bypass self-criticism and connect with possibility. Placing one "brave" image inside your "safe" space signals: I can grow without abandoning myself. This balance between grounding and stretching is key for trauma recovery, resilience, and lasting change.

Collect Images — Use magazines, printouts, or sketches. On the Safe side, paste images that represent rest, comfort, and security. On the Brave side, add images that symbolize courage, growth, or edges you dream of touching.

The Bridge Step — Choose one tiny image of bravery and place it into the Safe half. This represents your next gentle edge — a stretch that doesn't abandon your grounding.

Reflect — Ask yourself: What's one small way I can practice this edge this wee

SAFE	BRAVE

ACTION

EMOTIONS IN COLOR

Emotions can feel abstract or overwhelming when we only experience them as "stress" or "sadness." Adding color and body mapping turns them into something tangible, something you can see, name, and notice. This makes emotional awareness less scary and more approachable. By shading intensity and locating the sensations in your body, you start to recognize patterns, triggers, and areas that need extra care. This is not about judging the feeling — it's about mapping your internal landscape so you can respond with awareness rather than autopilot. Over time, it builds clarity, emotional literacy, and the ability to intervene with skillful action before overwhelm takes over.

Pick Colors — Assign a color to each emotion that feels right for you.
Shade Intensity — Color each wedge to reflect how strongly you feel that emotion today.
Body Mapping — Next to the wheel, jot where in your body each emotion lives (chest tightness, stomach flutter, jaw tension).
Reflect — Notice patterns, imbalances, or surprises. Consider one small action to soothe or honor a strong area.

SECTION TWO

The Unspoken Weight of Guilt and Shame

Guilt and shame are two of the most common yet complex emotions experienced after abortion. It's possible that, even though you made the decision you felt was best for you, these feelings still linger. Guilt may feel like an internal punishment—a belief that you've done something wrong, even if your choice was made from a place of necessity. Shame, on the other hand, might tell you that you are wrong or unworthy at your core—that your worth is tied to your decision. These emotions don't just affect how you view the choice you made; they can distort your sense of self and how you relate to others.

It's important to recognize that guilt and shame don't make you a bad person—they're just human responses to loss, societal judgment, and the complexities of choice. This section will guide you through understanding where these feelings come from, how they show up in your life, and how you can begin to free yourself from their hold. Healing begins with acknowledging these emotions and learning how to separate them from your true worth.

Making Sense Of It
The Roots and Weight of Shame After Abortion

Shame after abortion doesn't come out of nowhere. It grows from the soil of messages we've absorbed all our lives — about motherhood, sacrifice, gender roles, morality, and what it supposedly means to be "good." These scripts are so ingrained that even if you made the most thoughtful, necessary choice for yourself, you may still feel a heavy ache of having done something "wrong." Sometimes it isn't your own voice accusing you — it's the voices of family, culture, religion, or even broader societal silence. That silence, the lack of ritual or acknowledgment, makes grief harder to process because it leaves you carrying it alone. When you can't name your pain out loud without fear of judgment, shame multiplies in the dark.

It's important to distinguish between guilt and shame. Guilt says, "I did something wrong." Shame says, "I am wrong." After abortion, guilt might attach itself to the decision itself, but shame goes deeper, attacking your identity, your worthiness, even your right to grieve. This is why abortion grief can feel so layered and isolating — it isn't just sadness over what was lost. It's a battle with the story you've been told about who you are now.

What's more, shame after abortion isn't purely personal — it's systemic. Historically, women's bodies have been framed as vessels for others' expectations: family lineage, cultural duty, religious obedience.

Making Sense Of It
The Roots and Weight of Shame After Abortion

When you make a choice about your body that contradicts those expectations, it can feel like you've broken some sacred, unwritten contract — even if it was the most compassionate choice for your reality. That inherited weight is not yours to carry, yet shame makes it feel fused to your identity.

Neurologically, shame is powerful because it registers in the same brain regions as physical pain. It's why a single cutting phrase like "You'll regret this forever" or "You killed your baby" can lodge inside you like a wound. The brain reads shame as threat, and the nervous system reacts with withdrawal, numbness, or hypervigilance — a constant scanning for judgment. Over time, this can distort relationships, making it harder to reach for comfort or trust that you're still worthy of being loved fully.

But here's the shift: shame is not evidence of wrongdoing. It's an echo of judgment, a reflection of societal discomfort projected onto you. And because shame thrives in secrecy, it loosens its grip in the light — when it is named, spoken, and held with compassion. Each time you say out loud, "I feel ashamed, but this does not define me," you create a crack in the armor shame built around you. Healing isn't about erasing the memory of your decision. It's about reclaiming your sense of worth and separating yourself from the cultural and emotional weight that was unfairly handed to you. You did not fail. You are not broken. And you are not alone in carrying this.

What does guilt feel like for me in the context of my abortion?

Take a moment to reflect on what guilt feels like in your body and mind. Does it show up as a heavy feeling in your chest or a tightness in your stomach? How do you experience guilt when you think about your decision? Write about how it manifests for you. Recognize that the guilt you feel is an emotional response, not a permanent judgment of who you are.

What does guilt feel like for me in the context of my abortion?

What messages did I internalize about abortion, guilt, or shame growing up?

Think about what you were taught or exposed to regarding abortion and women's choices. Were there moral, religious, or societal beliefs that have shaped how you view your decision? Write about any messages you absorbed from family, culture, or media, and consider how those beliefs might be influencing your grief today.

What messages did I internalize about abortion, guilt, or shame growing up?

In what ways has shame affected how I see myself or relate to others?

Shame can be very isolating. Have you noticed ways in which shame might have caused you to withdraw from others or hide parts of yourself? Reflect on how shame has shaped your relationships or self-identity. Give yourself permission to see where shame has taken root and how it might be affecting your present life.

In what ways has shame affected how I see myself or relate to others?

How can I separate my worth from the decisions I've made?

It's easy to let decisions define who we are, but your worth is not based on one choice or action. Take a moment to reflect on your intrinsic value, beyond the grief or guilt you're feeling. What are the qualities that make you a good person? How can you remind yourself that your worth is not dependent on your past decisions?

How can I separate my worth from the decisions I've made?

What would I say to a friend who was feeling guilty or ashamed for having an abortion?

Imagine someone you care about has gone through the same experience. What words of kindness, compassion, and support would you offer them? Take a moment to write those words down. When guilt or shame arises in your own heart, refer back to this list to remind yourself that you are deserving of the same compassion.

What would I say to a friend who was feeling guilty or ashamed for having an abortion?

TRACING THE TRUTH

SHAME EXTERNALIZATION

Shame thrives in silence and secrecy. It convinces you that it is you. But shame is not your identity — it's a learned response, shaped by external voices and cultural messages. Naming it out loud creates distance and helps you reclaim yourself from it.

Why it helps:
Externalizing shame makes it visible and separate from your identity. It reminds you that while shame visits you, it doesn't define you.

Write a letter to your shame as if it were a person. Give it a voice and a personality. (Example: "You come in late at night when I'm most tired. **You whisper things that sound true but aren't.** You've borrowed the voices of people who never understood me.")
End the letter by setting a boundary with it. (Example: "You are not me. You don't get to decide who I am.")

If it feels safe, read the letter aloud or tear it up as a ritual of release.

TRACING THE TRUTH

SHAME EXTERNALIZATION

TRACING THE TRUTH

SHAME EXTERNALIZATION

TRACING THE TRUTH

COMPASSIONATE REFRAMING OF GUILT

Guilt often lingers as a voice telling you that you've done something wrong — even when your choice was made from necessity, survival, or care. What guilt rarely acknowledges is the context: the impossible decisions, the lack of resources, the competing realities that shaped your path.

Why it helps:
Reframing doesn't erase guilt overnight, but it interrupts the spiral of self-blame by bringing context and compassion back into the narrative. Over time, it weakens guilt's grip and makes room for truth.

Write down one guilt statement you often hear in your mind (e.g., "I shouldn't have chosen abortion").
Underneath it, write three compassionate reframes that tell the whole story. For example:
"I made the best decision I could with the circumstances I had."
"I chose with love for myself and for the life I was living."
"My decision does not erase my worthiness or my humanity."
Read your reframes aloud once a day for a week, even if your body resists believing them at first.

TRACING THE TRUTH

COMPASSIONATE REFRAMING OF GUILT

Guilty Statement:

Compassionate Reframing:

MOOD MAPPING BY THE HOUR

Our mood is never random — it's deeply influenced by what we do, when we do it, and how our nervous system responds. When depression or anxiety is heavy, it can feel like nothing makes a difference. This log helps you prove to yourself that even small activities shift your emotional state, sometimes by just one point. And that one-point lift matters — it's momentum, a reminder that you aren't stuck forever. By tracking your mood alongside your activities, you build a personalized map of what nourishes you. Instead of relying on guesswork, you'll have hard evidence of your own resilience patterns. Over time, this practice shows you that certain choices (a call with a safe friend, a walk outside, finishing a task) consistently bring relief. This isn't about forcing happiness — it's about noticing what gently nudges you toward better.

For one day, each hour, write down what you're doing and your mood (0–10).

Repeat for a few days — notice patterns.

Circle activities that reliably lift you by at least one point.

Intentionally schedule more of those "one-point lifts" into your week.

Revisit the log whenever you feel stuck, to remind yourself you have options.

Day	Activity	Mood Before	Mood After

ACTION

MOOD MAPPING BY THE HOUR

Day	Activity	Mood Before	Mood After

SELF-COMPASSION BREAK

When stress, shame, or pain flare up, most of us go straight into self-criticism: Why can't I handle this better? What's wrong with me? That inner attack only tightens the spiral. Kristin Neff's Self-Compassion Break interrupts that cycle. It gives you three small handholds: recognition of your pain, the reminder you're not alone in it, and an active choice to soften instead of harden against yourself. With repetition, your nervous system learns that you don't have to white-knuckle through suffering or numb out — you can meet yourself with the same tenderness you'd extend to a friend. That shift doesn't erase the pain, but it changes the way it lands in your body. Over time, it builds resilience, because you're no longer abandoned in hard moments; you become your own safe ally.

Notice —
Pause and acknowledge: "This is hard. This hurts."

Kindness —
Place a hand on your chest or cheek and whisper: "May I be gentle with myself right now."

Common Humanity —
Say: "Others feel this too. I'm not the only one struggling."

POCKET MOOD LIFTERS

When life feels heavy, it's easy to forget what actually helps. In hard moments, the brain tends to focus on what's wrong, not what's available. An Antidote List is your preloaded reminder: ten small, proven things that shift your state even a little. These aren't grand fixes or instant cures — they're micro-adjustments that keep you from sliding deeper into the stuckness. Pairing an antidote before a hard task helps you face it with steadier energy; using one after provides recovery and closure so you don't carry the weight forward. Over time, this list becomes muscle memory — your nervous system learns, When I struggle, I have options. That's the opposite of hopelessness.

1 **List Ten** — Write down 10 things that reliably lift your mood (a song, a walk, fresh air, texting a safe friend, lighting a candle). Keep them small and doable.

....

....

....

....

....

....

....

2 **Use Before** — Pick one before facing a task you tend to dread. Let it soften resistance.

3 **Use After** — Choose another as a closing ritual. Let it tell your body, That part is done. I'm safe again.

SECTION THREE

Reclaiming Your Power and Autonomy

When you experience grief after abortion, it's easy for your sense of power to feel lost. The weight of societal stigma, judgment from others, and the internalized guilt or shame can create the illusion that you've been stripped of your autonomy—like your decision was forced, rather than chosen. But your autonomy is your birthright. It's your power to make decisions that are in alignment with your needs, values, and well-being. No one, not even yourself, can take that power away unless you let it.

Reclaiming your power starts with recognizing that you always had the right to make this decision, regardless of the external pressures you may have faced. In this section, we'll explore how you can reconnect with the strength and autonomy that are yours by nature. We'll also look at how your power shows up in your body, your emotions, and your relationships. Healing begins when you remember that you are not powerless, and that you have the authority to live your life on your own terms.

Making Sense Of It
Taking Back What Was Always Yours

After abortion, it's common to feel like your autonomy slipped through your fingers — as if the weight of stigma, silence, and other people's expectations has rewritten your story for you. Even if you knew, deep down, that your decision was the right one, grief can tangle with guilt and leave you second-guessing everything. You may replay the circumstances, the conversations, the "what-ifs," until your choice feels less like something you owned and more like something that just happened to you. This is the cruel trick of shame: it tries to erase the fact that you had power all along.

But here's the truth: autonomy isn't erased by difficulty, or by grief, or by the fact that you wish life had given you different options. Autonomy is exercised in the very act of deciding — in choosing within the messy, complicated reality of your life. It doesn't mean you had every option available, or that the choice was painless. It means you acted from a place of self-awareness and survival, even when the world wanted to deny you that dignity.

The hardest part is that abortion grief often happens in silence. Society isn't set up to validate your complexity. Instead, you might face one of two extremes: people who condemn your choice, or people who dismiss it as "no big deal." Neither makes room for the layered truth — that your decision may have been both necessary and heartbreaking, both grounded and complicated. And when no one reflects back that truth, you can start to lose faith in your own voice.

Making Sense Of It
Taking Back What Was Always Yours

Reclaiming autonomy is the act of taking your voice back from all those external forces — the cultural scripts, the religious teachings, the political noise, the family expectations. It's asking, What was actually mine? What belonged to me in that moment? And when you peel away the layers of judgment, what you often find is that the core of your decision was rooted in love: love for yourself, love for your future, love for the people you care for, or even love for the baby you weren't able to welcome.

This isn't about glorifying the decision or minimizing the pain. It's about recognizing that you did not betray yourself. You acted with agency in the face of impossibility. And that is autonomy in its truest form.

On a deeper level, reclaiming your autonomy is also about learning to live inside your body again. Grief can make you feel estranged from yourself — as though your body carries a story you don't want to claim. But healing requires reconnection. Your body is not your enemy; it is the vessel of your resilience. Each time you breathe into your own truth, each time you recognize I had a say in this, you're repairing the fractured trust between you and your body, between you and your story.

Autonomy is not something anyone gave you. It was never theirs to grant. It has always been yours — and part of healing is remembering that no loss, no grief, and no judgment can take it away.

What does "power" mean to me in the context of my abortion?

Think about the moments when you felt empowered to make your decision, even if it was hard or conflicted. Was it the sense of self-preservation, the need to prioritize your well-being, or the choice to honor your personal circumstances? Reflect on what power looked like for you at the time, and what it feels like now in hindsight. How can you redefine what power means to you?

What does "power" mean to me in the context of my abortion?

When have I felt empowered in my life, even before my abortion?

Recall times in your life when you felt strong, capable, and in control. Perhaps it was during a difficult period where you had to stand firm in your decisions. Write about a time when you felt confident and certain in your ability to handle challenges. Reflect on how you can tap into that power now.

When have I felt empowered in my life, even before my abortion?

How has external judgment influenced my perception of my autonomy?

Consider how societal or familial expectations have shaped your understanding of autonomy. Have you ever felt that others' opinions about you or your choices diminished your own sense of agency? Write about any external pressures you may have internalized, and how you can begin to separate those from your own sense of what is right for you.

How has external judgment influenced my perception of my autonomy?

In what ways have I already exercised personal agency and resilience through this journey?

Take a moment to reflect on how you have shown up for yourself throughout your experience. Maybe you sought out counseling, made difficult but necessary decisions, or navigated complicated emotions. Write about the ways in which you've already demonstrated resilience and strength, even when it felt hard.

In what ways have I already exercised personal agency and resilience through this journey?

What does reclaiming my autonomy look like today?

Reclaiming your power doesn't just happen in the past—it's an ongoing process. What small actions can you take today to honor your sense of agency and autonomy? It might involve setting boundaries, making a decision that prioritizes your needs, or simply giving yourself permission to feel whole again. Write about what steps you can take to bring yourself back into the driver's seat of your life.

What does reclaiming my autonomy look like today?

TRACING THE TRUTH

SEPARATING THE VOICES

After abortion, it's easy for outside voices — family, religion, culture, politics — to tangle with your own, until you're not sure what's yours and what isn't. This exercise helps you separate those voices so you can hear your truth more clearly.

Why it helps:
This exercise helps you untangle shame from truth. It clarifies what belongs to you and what doesn't, giving you a clear sense of ownership over your story.

Under Not Mine, write down the messages or judgments you've absorbed from others (e.g., "Good people don't make this choice," "I should have done something differently").
Under Mine, write what you actually know or believe about your decision (e.g., "I made the choice I could with the life I had," "I acted with love for myself and others").
Cross out or circle each "Not Mine" voice to symbolically release it. Place a star beside the "Mine" statements that feel most grounding.

TRACING THE TRUTH

SEPARATING THE VOICES

Not Mine   **Mine**

TRACING THE TRUTH

WRITING A DECLARATION OF AUTONOMY

Sometimes the most radical act of healing is to declare your own authority out loud. This exercise helps you reclaim your voice by crafting a personal declaration of autonomy that you can return to whenever shame or doubt resurfaces.

Why it helps:
Putting your truth into words creates a touchstone. It's not about convincing yourself you feel only peace — it's about reclaiming authority over your narrative, again and again, until it sinks into your bones.

On a blank page, write the sentence: "This was my decision, and here is what I want to remember about it..."
Continue writing, naming the truths you want to anchor in — the circumstances you faced, the love or necessity behind your choice, the strength it took to follow through.
End with a statement of reclamation, such as: "My autonomy is mine. My story is mine. I refuse to hand them over again."

TRACING THE TRUTH

WRITING A DECLARATION OF AUTONOMY

TRACING THE TRUTH

WRITING A DECLARATION OF AUTONOMY

ACTION

HOLDING HARD DATES

When difficult anniversaries come around—whether it's the day everything fell apart, a loss, or a traumatic turning point—the body remembers even when the mind tries not to. This can show up as anxiety, fatigue, irritability, or old grief bubbling back. Creating an intentional ritual allows you to meet those days with structure instead of being blindsided. By noting the date ahead of time, building in gentle scaffolding (like a support person, a nourishing activity, and less demand on yourself), you create a container for your nervous system. Closing the day with gratitude is not about being thankful for the pain itself, but for your endurance—that you lived through it, and you're still here. Ritual turns an overwhelming anniversary into a moment of honoring resilience.

Mark the Date
Note the anniversary on your calendar so it doesn't sneak up.

Plan Support
Choose one person you can reach out to if things feel heavy.

Nourish
Schedule at least one grounding or soothing activity (walk, bath, journaling, cozy meal).

Lighten the Load
Keep your to-do list small that day.

Close with Gratitude
End the evening by writing or saying one thing you're grateful for in your survival.

ACTION

SAFETY IN SENSATION

After stress, trauma, or relational upheaval, our bodies often feel like a battleground—tense, guarded, or disconnected. Reclaiming the body is about coming back home to yourself. By practicing gentle, nurturing touch, you signal to your nervous system that it's safe to soften. This isn't indulgence; it's essential care. Daily attention to your physical self strengthens body awareness, lowers chronic tension, and reminds you that your body is a safe place, not just a vessel for pain. Over time, these small acts become proof: I can care for myself, and my body can be trusted again.

1 — PICK A NURTURING TOUCH
Examples include rubbing lotion into your hands, sinking into a warm bath, wearing soft or comforting clothes, or even a gentle hand on your chest.

2 — ENGAGE FULLY
Notice textures, warmth, weight, or scents — bring mindful awareness to the sensation.

3 — BREATHE INTO THE TOUCH
Let each inhale gather calm, each exhale release tension.

4 — PRACTICE DAILY
Even 2–5 minutes consistently signals safety and care.

5 — NOTICE CHANGES
Check in with your body and note any softening, release, or increased comfort over time.

ACTION

SAFETY IN SENSATION

After stress, trauma, or relational upheaval, our bodies often feel like a battleground—tense, guarded, or disconnected. Reclaiming the body is about coming back home to yourself. By practicing gentle, nurturing touch, you signal to your nervous system that it's safe to soften. This isn't indulgence; it's essential care. Daily attention to your physical self strengthens body awareness, lowers chronic tension, and reminds you that your body is a safe place, not just a vessel for pain. Over time, these small acts become proof: I can care for myself, and my body can be trusted again.

1. PICK A NURTURING TOUCH
Examples include rubbing lotion into your hands, sinking into a warm bath, wearing soft or comforting clothes, or even a gentle hand on your chest.

2. ENGAGE FULLY
Notice textures, warmth, weight, or scents — bring mindful awareness to the sensation.

3. BREATHE INTO THE TOUCH
Let each inhale gather calm, each exhale release tension.

4. PRACTICE DAILY
Even 2–5 minutes consistently signals safety and care.

5. NOTICE CHANGES
Check in with your body and note any softening, release, or increased comfort over time.

WORRY WINDOW

Worries often hijack your mind, showing up at every unexpected moment. By giving them a dedicated "time slot," you reclaim control instead of letting them run your day. This practice teaches your nervous system that there's a safe space and a safe time to process, so you're not constantly reacting to every intrusive thought. During the window, you can gently evaluate what's actionable versus what you need to let go, building clarity and self-trust. Outside the window, a simple cue like "not now—later" helps you return to the present without guilt or shame. Over time, this simple structure reduces the intensity and frequency of anxious loops.

Park your worries: Write them down as they arise.

....

....

....

....

Set a 15-minute window: Choose a consistent time each day for processing.

....

Outside the window: Use a cue phrase like "not now—later" to return to your day.

Inside the window: Review the list. Solve what's actionable, accept what isn't, and release judgment.

Close the window: End with a grounding or soothing activity to signal completion.

GENTLE BREATH FOCUS

When anxiety spikes, the mind and body race together — thoughts accelerate, heart rate climbs, muscles tighten. Counting your breath gives both something steady to follow. By pairing inhale and exhale with numbers, you create a gentle anchor that slows the nervous system, refocuses attention, and interrupts spiraling thoughts. This isn't about perfection or achieving ten — it's about returning to the rhythm whenever distraction occurs. Even a few minutes daily strengthens your capacity to notice tension, settle your body, and move through anxious moments with less overwhelm.

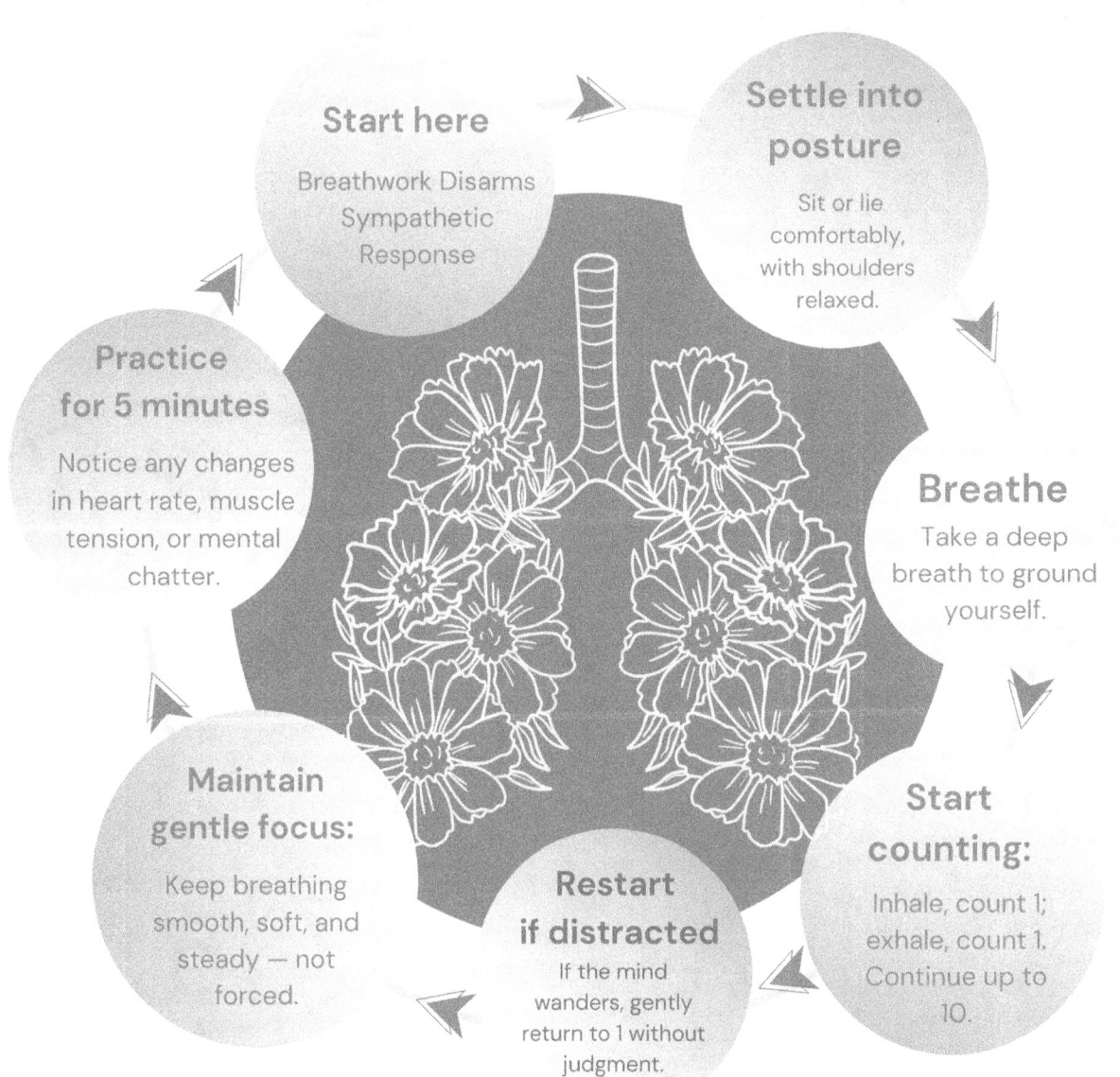

Start here
Breathwork Disarms Sympathetic Response

Settle into posture
Sit or lie comfortably, with shoulders relaxed.

Breathe
Take a deep breath to ground yourself.

Start counting:
Inhale, count 1; exhale, count 1. Continue up to 10.

Restart if distracted
If the mind wanders, gently return to 1 without judgment.

Maintain gentle focus:
Keep breathing smooth, soft, and steady — not forced.

Practice for 5 minutes
Notice any changes in heart rate, muscle tension, or mental chatter.

SECTION FOUR

Finding Peace with the Past

It's natural to look back on pivotal moments in life and wonder, "Did I make the right choice?" In the aftermath of abortion, it's easy to spiral into a cycle of regret, guilt, and "what ifs." The truth is, no decision, no matter how painful, should define your entire life. The past is fixed, but how we make peace with it shapes our present and future.

In this section, we'll explore the process of forgiving yourself and finding resolution, not by forgetting, but by reframing the past. You are not your decision, and the grief you feel doesn't diminish your worth or the validity of your choice. Learning to find peace with your past means honoring it—understanding why you made the decision you did, acknowledging the complexity of your feelings, and, most importantly, giving yourself permission to heal. It's a journey toward embracing the truth that you can move forward without being weighed down by the past.

Making Sense Of It

Making Peace Without Forgetting

Looking back after abortion can feel like walking through a hall of mirrors — each reflection showing a different "what if," a different self, a different outcome. Grief, guilt, and shame often layer over one another, creating the illusion that the past is a cage you cannot escape. Yet psychologically, the past only holds as much power as we give it. How we interpret and integrate our experiences determines whether they shape us as prisons or as guides.

One of the hardest truths is that decision-making in real life is never neat or purely rational. Choices are shaped by circumstance, resources, knowledge, emotion, and survival. Yet our culture often frames abortion as a moral "black-and-white" decision. When we internalize these external narratives, it's easy to replay our own story through a lens of judgment instead of context. This can make the mind ruminate endlessly — analyzing, blaming, or imagining a different timeline — which traps us in a loop of emotional distress.

Finding peace is not about erasing memory or forcing forgiveness before you're ready. It's about acknowledging complexity and reclaiming authorship of your narrative. It's recognizing that regret and grief do not negate agency. Neuroscience tells us that when we intentionally reframe memories — bringing compassion, context, and self-understanding — we activate neural pathways associated with emotional regulation and resilience.

Making Sense Of It
Making Peace Without Forgetting

By reframing, the brain learns to carry the story with less charge, integrating it into the broader tapestry of your life rather than leaving it as a raw, unprocessed wound.

Socially, peace also comes from recognizing that the judgment of others doesn't define your experience. Humans are embedded in culture, and the voices around us — family, friends, society — shape our emotional responses. When those voices conflict with our reality, shame and rumination intensify. Actively creating a compassionate internal dialogue, rooted in your own lived truth, counters these external pressures and restores a sense of authority over your life story.

Ultimately, finding peace is both an emotional and cognitive process. It allows grief to exist without letting it dominate your identity. It turns regret into reflection, and it transforms judgment into understanding. You are not your past decisions, and your worth is not contingent on external approval. By making space for complexity, you reclaim your life from the weight of the past and step forward with clarity, self-compassion, and renewed agency.

What does "forgiveness" mean to me in the context of my abortion experience?

Forgiveness can feel like a big word, especially when we're dealing with something as emotionally charged as abortion. But forgiveness doesn't mean excusing a decision or forgetting it. It means acknowledging that you did the best you could with the knowledge and resources you had at the time. Reflect on what forgiveness looks like for you. Can you extend it to yourself?

What does "forgiveness" mean to me in the context of my abortion experience?

What do I need to understand about the past in order to move forward?

Sometimes the past can hold us hostage, especially when we feel stuck in regret or confusion. Ask yourself: What do I need to understand in order to release my hold on the past? Do I need more compassion for myself, more clarity about my choices, or a deeper acceptance of my feelings? Take time to explore what you need from your past to feel at peace.

What do I need to understand about the past in order to move forward?

What are the stories I've told myself about my decision, and how can I reframe them with compassion?

Often, we have narratives in our minds that judge our choices harshly. Maybe the story you tell yourself about your abortion is one of regret, failure, or fear. What would it look like if you reframed that story with compassion and understanding? How could you view your decision with more kindness? Write about how you might shift your internal narrative.

What are the stories I've told myself about my decision, and how can I reframe them with compassion?

How can I show myself the same compassion I would offer a close friend in my situation?

Think about how you would respond if a friend came to you with the same experience. You would likely offer them warmth, validation, and understanding. Now, consider how you can extend those same gestures of compassion to yourself. Write about ways you can be kinder and more patient with yourself as you move through this healing journey.

How can I show myself the same compassion I would offer a close friend in my situation?

What would it look like to let go of guilt or regret, even just a little?

Guilt and regret are heavy burdens to carry, and often, they're linked to the belief that we could have or should have done something differently. Reflect on what it might feel like to let go of even a small part of that burden. What would happen if you allowed yourself to release some of the guilt or regret, if only for a moment?

What would it look like to let go of guilt or regret, even just a little?

TRACING THE TRUTH

LETTER OF COMPASSION TO YOUR PAST SELF

Often, the hardest person to forgive is yourself. This exercise gives you the chance to speak to the version of you who made the choice — with empathy, validation, and acknowledgment of everything they were navigating.

Why it helps:
Writing directly to your past self externalizes the internal dialogue of self-judgment. It allows you to hold space for grief while introducing a compassionate perspective, fostering emotional integration and inner peace.

Begin a letter with: "Dear Me at [time of decision]..."
Reflect on the challenges, pressures, and emotions your past self faced.
Acknowledge the bravery, thoughtfulness, and humanity in the choice.
Offer compassion and understanding, writing as if you were speaking to a close friend. Examples: "I see how heavy that choice was for you. I know you acted with love and courage."
Close with a statement of acceptance, such as: "I hold you with care. I honor your experience. You are not defined by this moment alone."

TRACING THE TRUTH

LETTER OF COMPASSION TO YOUR PAST SELF

TRACING THE TRUTH

LETTER OF COMPASSION TO YOUR PAST SELF

TRACING THE TRUTH

LETTER OF COMPASSION TO YOUR PAST SELF

TRACING THE TRUTH

TIMELINE OF UNDERSTANDING

Looking back can feel overwhelming, especially when regret and "what ifs" keep circling. This exercise creates a visual way to contextualize your decision, your feelings, and your growth over time — helping you see your past not as a fixed point of failure, but as part of a larger, evolving story.

Why it helps:
Seeing your past visually helps you integrate context, feelings, and growth. It reframes the decision as part of a human, complex experience rather than a moral failing, fostering understanding and self-compassion.

Draw a horizontal line across a page to represent your life. Mark the point when the abortion occurred.
Above the line, write the external pressures, circumstances, or context that influenced your decision. This can include financial realities, relationships, personal health, or cultural expectations.
Below the line, write your feelings and internal experience at the time — grief, relief, fear, or love.

On the next page, write a reflection on how that experience has shaped your resilience, self-knowledge, or values today.

TRACING THE TRUTH

TIMELINE OF UNDERSTANDING

TRACING THE TRUTH

TIMELINE OF UNDERSTANDING

ROOT YOURSELF

When stress or overwhelm hits, our nervous system often leaves us feeling unsteady, scattered, or "light-headed" in our own body. Imagining roots growing from your feet into the earth reconnects your body and mind, giving your nervous system a tangible sense of stability. Sending tension down those roots with your exhale encourages your body to release stress physically, not just mentally. Even a minute or two can create a noticeable sense of calm and grounding.

01 STAND OR SIT
with feet flat on the floor.

02 VISUALIZE ROOTS
extending from the soles of your feet into the earth.

03 ON EACH EXHALE
imagine tension or tightness flowing down the roots.

04 CONTINUE FOR 1–3 MINUTES
noticing the sense of weight, stability, and calm building in your body.

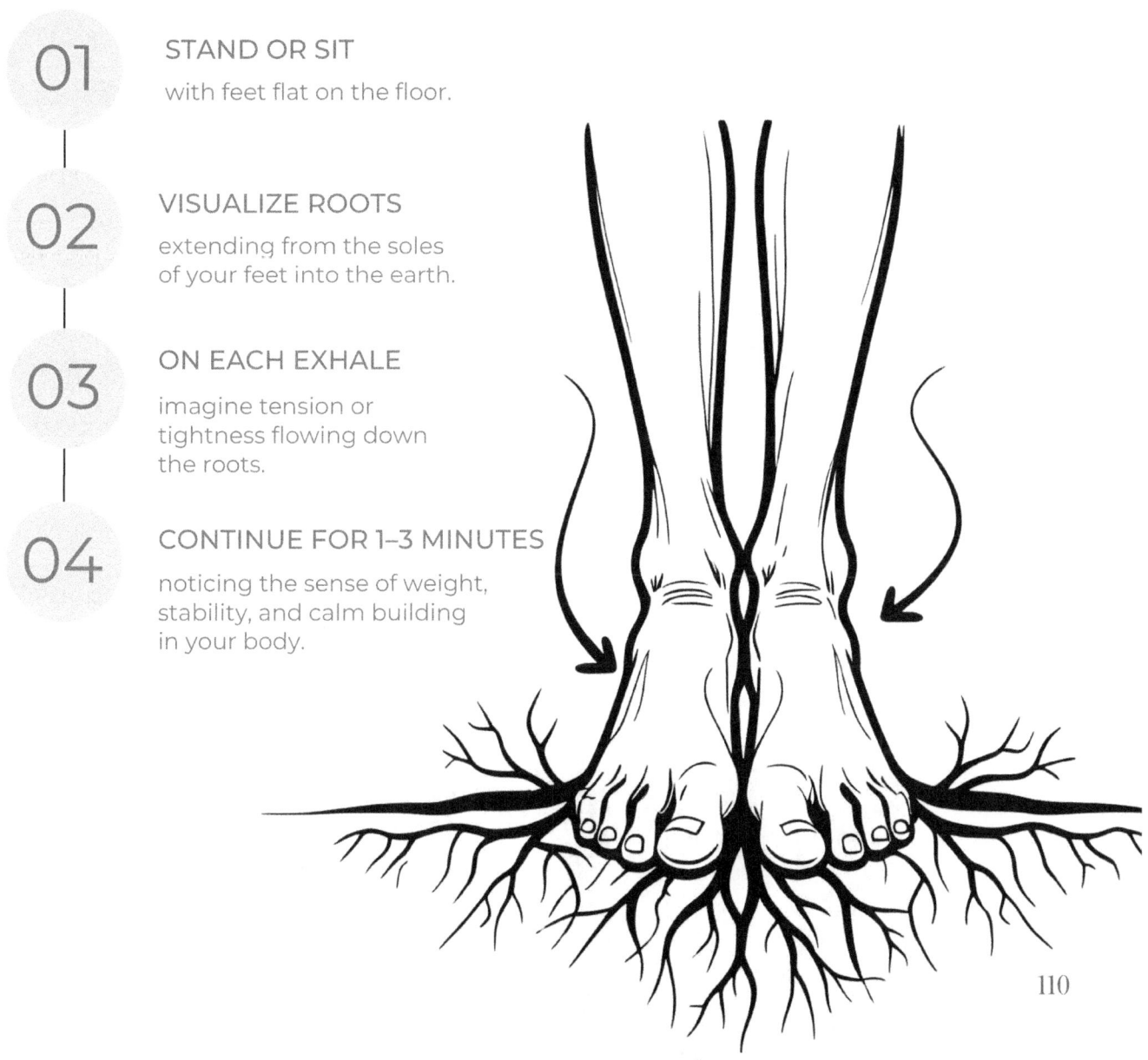

ACTION

ORIENTATION

When anxiety or overwhelm spikes, the mind and body can feel unmoored, as if you're "floating" in your thoughts. Orientation gently reconnects you with your environment, reminding your nervous system that you are safe in this moment. Slowly scanning your surroundings with your eyes and naming what you notice allows your body to register the present physically, which can reduce hypervigilance, grounding you in both sight and sensation.

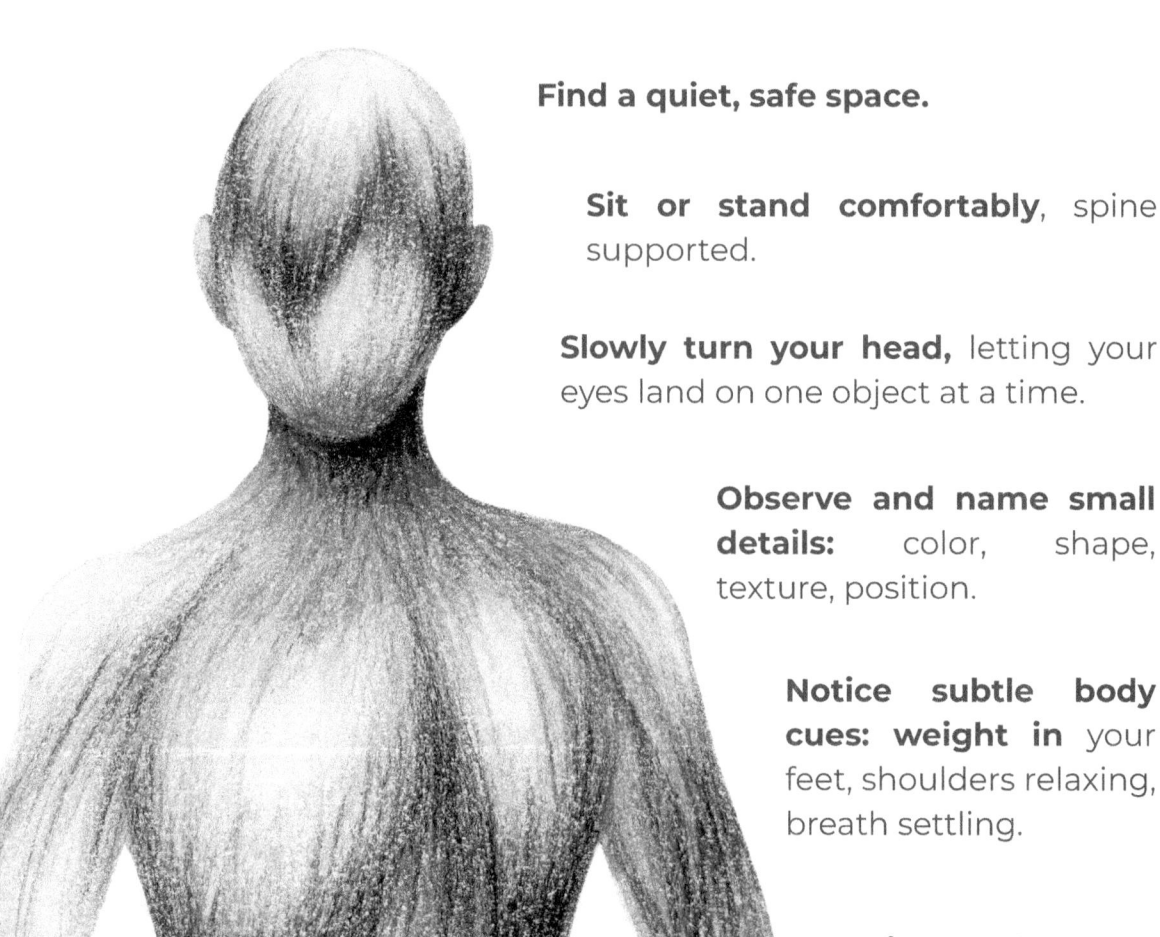

Find a quiet, safe space.

Sit or stand comfortably, spine supported.

Slowly turn your head, letting your eyes land on one object at a time.

Observe and name small details: color, shape, texture, position.

Notice subtle body cues: weight in your feet, shoulders relaxing, breath settling.

Continue for 1–2 minutes, allowing yourself to feel "here and now."

ACTION

SHOULDER RELEASE BREATH

Tension often hides in the shoulders, jaw, and forehead when stress or overwhelm is high. Pairing a deep inhale with a long audible sigh signals the nervous system that it's safe to release. Dropping the shoulders with each exhale creates a physical cue for letting go, while checking the jaw and forehead increases bodily awareness, helping you notice where stress lingers. This simple practice offers a mini reset, reducing tension and signaling calm without overthinking.

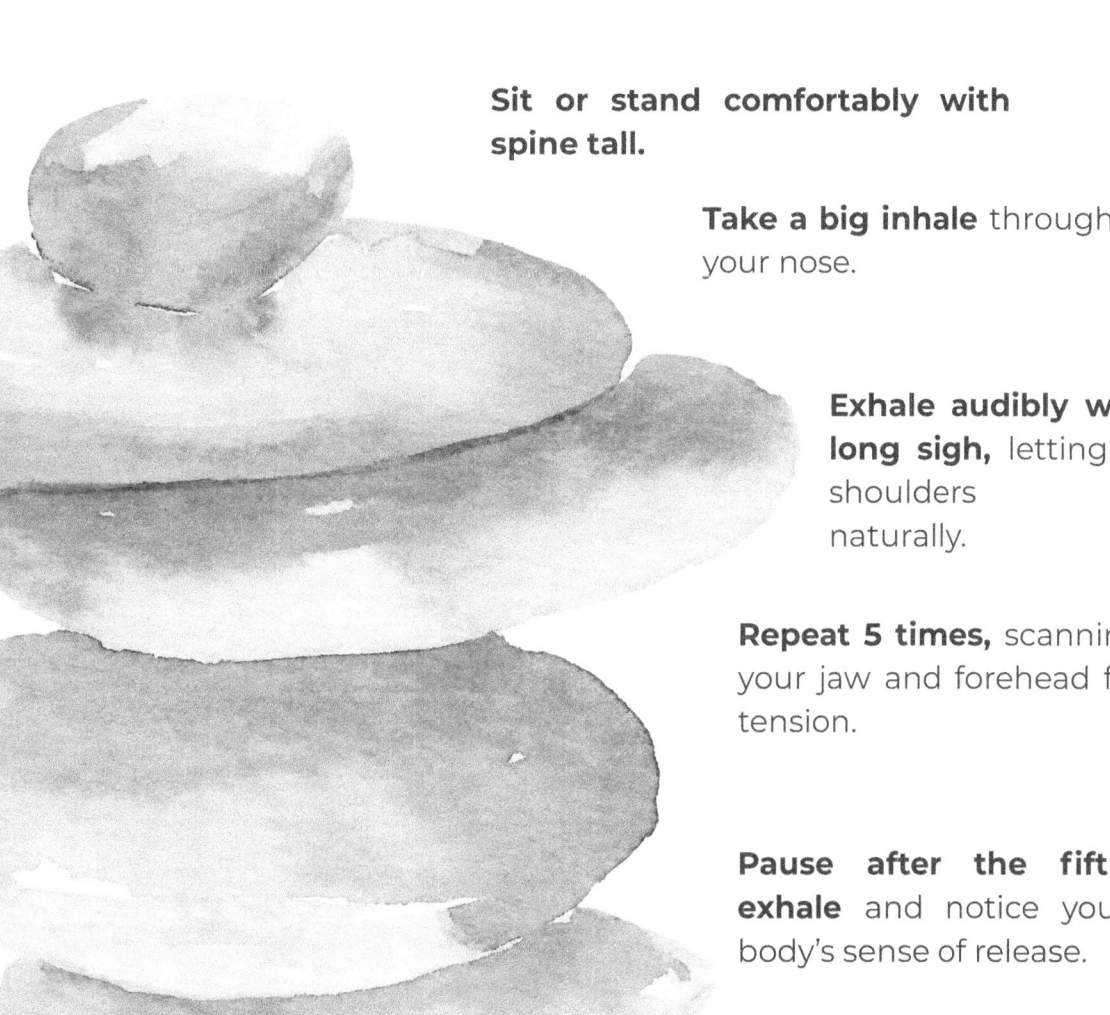

Sit or stand comfortably with spine tall.

Take a big inhale through your nose.

Exhale audibly with a long sigh, letting your shoulders drop naturally.

Repeat 5 times, scanning your jaw and forehead for tension.

Pause after the fifth exhale and notice your body's sense of release.

ACTION

PROTECTIVE BUBBLE

When emotions run high or interactions feel draining, it's easy for your energy to get scattered. Imagining a soft, light bubble around you helps create a sense of personal space and safety. Using your breath to strengthen the bubble on the inhale and filter in only what feels nourishing on the exhale trains your nervous system to notice boundaries, giving you a calm, centered feeling even in challenging situations.

Sit or stand comfortably, spine tall.

Visualize a soft bubble surrounding your body, glowing lightly.

Inhale and imagine the bubble strengthening, expanding slightly.

Exhale and let in only what nourishes — warmth, safety, or calm.

Continue for 1–3 minutes, noticing a sense of energetic protection and centeredness.

SECTION FIVE

Reclaiming Your Power

After abortion, it can sometimes feel like everything is out of your hands—your body, your emotions, your future. It's easy to get caught in a spiral of shame or doubt, believing that you no longer have control over your life. But the truth is, you have immense power within you. Power to heal. Power to rebuild. Power to define what your life looks like moving forward.

In this section, we're going to focus on reclaiming your personal power. This isn't about erasing the past; it's about reconnecting with the part of you that is strong, resilient, and capable of change. You are not defined by a single choice or moment in time. Your ability to heal and move forward rests in your hands. Together, we'll explore how you can take back control over your narrative, your emotions, and your future.

Making Sense Of It
Reconnecting with Your Inner Authority

Abortion grief can leave you feeling fragmented — as if the very act of choosing created a crack between who you were, who you are, and who you hope to be. When life hands us decisions that carry weight, our sense of control can feel suspended, leaving us vulnerable to shame, doubt, and self-questioning. But power isn't the absence of difficulty; it's the ability to act in the face of it, and to reclaim agency over your own narrative.

Psychologically, reclaiming power after abortion requires distinguishing between the elements of your experience that were imposed on you — societal pressures, judgment, misinformation — and the elements that were truly yours: your values, your reasoning, your heart. This is a deeply human process: it demands honesty with yourself, curiosity about your own motivations, and courage to claim ownership of your life again. Autonomy and empowerment aren't abstract ideals; they are built in the small, deliberate acts of saying, "This is my body, my choice, my story."

Socially and culturally, many people internalize messages that their power is conditional. Women, in particular, are often told that authority over their bodies or choices comes with limits, and stepping outside these invisible rules can trigger guilt or anxiety. Reclaiming power is, in part, a rebellion against these constraints. It's a conscious decision to stop letting external narratives dictate your sense of worth, value, or capability.

Making Sense Of It
Reconnecting with Your Inner Authority

On a somatic level, power is embodied. Grief and trauma can leave tension in the body, constriction in the chest, or heaviness in the limbs — all physical markers of disempowerment. Reclaiming your power means reactivating these channels: breathing deeply, aligning posture, feeling your feet grounded, and connecting with the sense of capability that resides within your body. Healing the mind without acknowledging the body leaves empowerment incomplete.

Ultimately, reclaiming power after abortion is a multidimensional act: it's mental, emotional, social, and physical. It's acknowledging the complexity of your grief while refusing to let it define your future. It's understanding that while the world may have tried to dictate the terms of your life, the authority to shape what comes next has always been, and will always remain, in your hands.

What parts of my life do I feel powerless in right now?

Identify the areas in your life where you feel a loss of control. Is it in your emotions, your future, your relationships? Write about these feelings of powerlessness. How do they show up in your daily life? And more importantly, where can you begin to reclaim even the smallest bit of control?

What parts of my life do I feel powerless in right now?

What is one choice I can make today to regain some of my power?

Power isn't just about grand gestures; it's about the small, consistent choices we make each day. Think of one thing you can do today—no matter how small—that will give you a sense of agency. Maybe it's setting a boundary, saying "no" to something, or taking time for self-care. Write about this choice and how it feels to step into your own power.

What is one choice I can make today to regain some of my power?

What strengths have I discovered in myself through this experience?

Every challenge we face reveals something new about our inner strength. What have you learned about yourself during this journey? Have you discovered resilience, compassion, or courage in places you didn't expect? Reflect on the strengths you've uncovered and how they can support you as you move forward.

What strengths have I discovered in myself through this experience?

What are the things I feel guilty about, and how can I begin to release them?

Guilt can drain our energy and sense of power. Write about the things you feel guilty for—whether it's your decision, the grief you carry, or anything else. Now, reflect on how you can start releasing that guilt. What would it look like to forgive yourself or allow yourself to let go, even just a little?

What are the things I feel guilty about, and how can I begin to release them?

What does "taking control" of my life mean in this moment?

Reclaiming power means defining what control looks like for you, right now. This is not about perfection but about taking small steps toward ownership over your life. Reflect on what it means to take control today—whether it's how you react to your emotions, what boundaries you set, or how you approach your healing process.

What does "taking control" of my life mean in this moment?

TRACING THE TRUTH

THE CIRCLE OF AUTHORITY

When grief and societal judgment cloud your sense of control, it helps to visually map where your power truly lies. This exercise clarifies what you can influence and what belongs to others, so you can reclaim the authority that's always yours.

Why it helps:
This exercise externalizes control, showing the reader that authority and influence are not lost — they were never in the hands of others. It fosters clarity, groundedness, and a renewed sense of self-directed action.

Around this circle, write everything you can control or influence — your choices, your reactions, your boundaries, your healing practices, your body, your narrative.
Outside the circle, write everything that is not yours to control — other people's judgments, societal expectations, the past, others' reactions.

Reflect: notice how much power you already hold within the circle, and how releasing what's outside frees you from unnecessary burden.

TRACING THE TRUTH

DECLARATION OF POWER

Words shape perception, and speaking your truth aloud strengthens your sense of agency. This exercise helps solidify the reader's connection to their inner authority.

Why it helps:
Writing and repeating a declaration of power reinforces internal authority and autonomy. It bridges the mental, emotional, and somatic aspects of empowerment, grounding the reader in their right to steer their own healing journey.

Begin a written statement with: "I am the author of my life. My power belongs to me. I claim…"
Continue by naming concrete aspects of your life, body, or mind over which you can exercise control. Examples: "…the right to heal in my own way," "…the right to set boundaries," "…the right to honor my feelings without shame."
Close the declaration with a statement of ownership: "No one else can define my worth or my choices. My power is mine, now and always."

My Declaration

TRACING THE TRUTH

THE CIRCLE OF AUTHORITY

ACTION

LEAVES ON A STREAM

We often get stuck in our thoughts, treating them as commands or facts, which fuels stress and emotional overwhelm. Defusion teaches you to step back and see thoughts as just thoughts—mental events that come and go. By visualizing them on leaves drifting down a stream, you give your mind space to notice them without reacting. This practice reduces the pull of negative thinking, strengthens present-moment awareness, and improves emotional flexibility.

Sit quietly and settle. Take a few slow breaths, noticing your body and surroundings.

Visualize the stream. Picture a gentle stream flowing in front of you.

Place thoughts on leaves. Each time a thought appears, imagine putting it on a leaf floating by.

Label hooked moments. If you notice you're caught up in a thought, gently label it "thinking" and return it to the stream.

Continue for 5–10 minutes. Keep observing without judgment, letting each thought drift away.

ACTION

MOMENT-TO-MOMENT AWARENESS

Our minds are constantly busy—hearing, thinking, planning, feeling—and it's easy to get swept away in the stream of thoughts and sensations. This practice helps you step back and notice what's happening in the present without getting stuck. By softly labeling each experience, you create a gentle separation between yourself and the flood of mental activity. Even a short daily practice trains your attention, lowers emotional reactivity, and strengthens the ability to return to calm focus when life gets overwhelming.

Set a timer for 5 minutes so you can fully commit without checking the clock.

Sit comfortably and close your eyes if you like.

Notice experiences as they arise. Softly label them as: "hearing… thinking… planning… feeling…"

Return to your breath. After labeling, bring your attention back to your natural breathing.

Repeat gently. Whenever your mind wanders, notice it, label it, and return to the breath without judgment.

SECTION SIX

Embracing Your Healing Journey

Healing isn't linear. It doesn't follow a set path, nor does it happen according to any timeline. After an abortion, the journey to healing is deeply personal and unique, full of both progress and setbacks. You may feel like you've taken two steps forward, only to find yourself slipping backward in moments of grief or uncertainty. But that's okay. Healing isn't a destination; it's a process, a journey that unfolds at its own pace.

In this section, we're going to explore what it means to embrace your healing journey—without rushing, without judgment, and without the pressure to "get over it." Healing is about moving forward at your own pace, recognizing that each moment of pain or confusion is a part of your growth. You are not broken, and your healing will not be the same as anyone else's. The only thing that matters is that you allow yourself to heal, to grow, and to take the steps that feel right for you.

Making Sense Of It
Healing as a Rhythm, Not a Race

Healing after abortion challenges the way we think about progress, because grief is rarely linear. Our culture often frames recovery as a straight line: pain, reflection, closure, and "moving on." But the human mind, heart, and body do not heal in tidy sequences. Trauma and loss create ripples through cognition, emotion, and physiology, meaning that grief can resurface unpredictably, sometimes months or years after the decision. This is not a failure—it is the natural rhythm of healing.

Psychologically, embracing your journey involves recognizing the oscillation between movement and pause, reflection and action, sorrow and relief. The Dual Process Model of grief illustrates this beautifully: humans tend to shift between loss-oriented processes (facing grief, mourning, remembering) and restoration-oriented processes (resuming daily life, rebuilding routines, envisioning the future). Learning to move fluidly between these modes, rather than judging yourself for setbacks, strengthens resilience and fosters self-compassion.

Sociologically, the isolation that often accompanies abortion grief can intensify the feeling of being "stuck" or abnormal. People around you may expect closure on someone else's timeline or minimize the significance of your experience. When you internalize these external pressures, it can amplify shame or self-doubt, making moments of regression feel like failure.

Making Sense Of It
Healing as a Rhythm, Not a Race

Understanding that these reactions are socially conditioned, not inherent flaws, allows you to reframe setbacks as natural milestones in the broader arc of recovery.

Neuroscience also underscores the importance of patience in healing. Neural pathways tied to trauma and grief are deeply encoded; revisiting pain is part of reorganizing these networks. Each time you notice grief arising, pause, and respond with awareness, your brain gradually integrates the experience, reducing emotional volatility and increasing your capacity for presence and self-compassion.

Ultimately, embracing your healing journey is about reclaiming agency over your own pace and rhythm. It is choosing to honor your emotions without judgment, to move when ready, to pause when necessary, and to recognize that healing is a lifelong, evolving dialogue with yourself. The power lies not in how quickly you "recover," but in your willingness to stay present, grounded, and compassionate with your own experience. By letting go of rigid expectations, you cultivate a deep, authentic resilience that sustains both grief and growth, side by side.

What does healing look like for me right now?

Healing isn't about "getting over" your abortion but about finding peace and resolution in your own time. Reflect on what healing means for you, in this moment. Is it about acceptance? Self-forgiveness? Building new boundaries? Write about what healing feels like and looks like for you right now.

What does healing look like for me right now?

What are the emotions I'm afraid to feel, and why?

Sometimes, we resist certain emotions because they feel too overwhelming or too painful. Are there emotions you've been avoiding—grief, guilt, anger, or even relief? Reflect on why you might be avoiding them. What would happen if you allowed yourself to feel them? Write about the fear of feeling these emotions and what might shift if you allowed them to surface.

What are the emotions I'm afraid to feel, and why?

What does "patience" with myself look like?

Healing requires patience—not just with the process but with yourself. It's easy to be hard on yourself when you're struggling, but self-patience is a vital tool for emotional growth. What does being patient with yourself look like? Write about how you can embrace patience in your journey, even when it feels slow or uneven.

What does "patience" with myself look like?

What are the small steps I can take today toward healing?

Healing can feel overwhelming if you focus on the whole journey at once. Instead, break it down into small steps. What's one thing you can do today—whether it's journaling, setting a boundary, reaching out for support—that will help you feel like you're making progress? Write about this step and how it might impact your healing process.

What are the small steps I can take today toward healing?

How do I want to feel at the end of this journey?

Imagine yourself at the end of your healing journey. How do you want to feel? What kind of person do you want to be after you've moved through the pain and grief? Write about the future version of yourself and the emotional growth you want to experience.

How do I want to feel at the end of this journey?

TRACING THE TRUTH

CHECK-IN JOURNAL RITUAL

Regularly checking in with yourself strengthens awareness and encourages gentleness, helping you honor your pace rather than external expectations.

Why it helps:
This ritual builds consistent self-awareness and integrates the oscillation between loss and restoration. Over time, it strengthens emotional regulation, validates your experience, and reinforces that healing is a living, evolving process.

Set aside 5–10 minutes daily or weekly.
Answer three prompts:
What emotions am I feeling right now?
What small action or thought today helped me honor my healing?
Where do I need patience or compassion with myself today?

Close by taking three slow breaths, acknowledging both the grief and the growth present in this moment.

TRACING THE TRUTH

HEALING RHYTHM MAP

Healing isn't a straight line. This exercise helps you visualize the natural ups and downs of your journey, giving permission to experience both progress and setbacks without judgment.

Why it helps:
Mapping your rhythm visually reinforces that healing is nonlinear and validates both progress and regression. It shifts perspective from "I should be past this" to "I am moving through this," fostering patience and self-compassion.

Draw a wavy line across a page to represent your emotional and healing journey over the past weeks or months.
Mark the high points (moments of clarity, relief, or self-compassion) and low points (grief, guilt, or triggers).
For each high point, note what helped you feel grounded or resilient. For each low point, note what you learned about yourself or your needs.

Reflect on the overall pattern: notice the flow of healing, the oscillation between grief and restoration, and the resilience that persists through it all.

TRACING THE TRUTH

HEALING RHYTHM MAP

ACTION

EMOTION PAUSE & SHIFT

Emotions are powerful signals, but they don't always reflect the full truth of a situation. Sometimes anger, fear, or shame pushes us toward behaviors that make things worse—reacting sharply, withdrawing, or avoiding. Opposite Action gives you a way to step out of automatic emotional reactions and act in a way that aligns with your values and long-term well-being. By pausing, checking if the emotion is justified, and responding intentionally in the opposite direction, you teach your mind and body that you can handle emotions without letting them control you. Over time, this reduces emotional reactivity and strengthens self-trust.

Name the emotion and urge.

Example: Anger → yelling at someone.

Check the facts.

Is the intensity of the emotion justified by what actually happened, or is it amplified by past patterns, assumptions, or stress?

Choose the opposite behavior.

Act in a way that's constructive, compassionate, or gentle.
Example: Use a calm tone, approach the person respectfully, or step away for a mindful pause.

Stay with the emotion.

Continue the opposite behavior until the intensity drops by about half. Notice how your body and mind respond differently.

ACTION

NERVOUS SYSTEM RESET

Sometimes your body gets stuck in high alert—heart racing, muscles tight, mind spiraling—and it's hard to think or respond clearly. TIP Skills target the physiology directly, calming your nervous system so your emotions have space to settle. Using temperature, movement, and breathing strategically helps you interrupt the stress response, release adrenaline, and regain a sense of control. This isn't about ignoring feelings—it's about resetting your body so you can respond thoughtfully instead of reacting out of overwhelm.

T =
TEMPERATURE

I =
INTENSE EXERCISE

P =
PACED BREATHING

P =
PROGRESSIVE MUSCLE RELAXATION

Splash cool water on your face or neck, or use a cold pack. This signals your body that it's safe to downshift.

Create several posts of the same type at once, schedule them using an app, and upload them so they are available at the right time

You can save time by copying and pasting the CTA into your posts instead of writing it out again every time

Create some posts with a frame around your branding image. You can reuse the same image after at least 9 posts but change the brand colour for a different look

SECTION SEVEN

Healing Through Connection

Grief can feel incredibly isolating, especially when you're navigating complex emotions after an abortion. The feelings of sadness, regret, and confusion can create a sense of distance from others, or even from yourself. It might feel like you're carrying a burden that no one else can truly understand. In those moments, it's important to remember that healing is rarely a solitary journey. It thrives in the safety of connection—whether with others who offer compassion and understanding or with yourself, through self-compassion and reflection.

This section is about the power of connection: how nurturing relationships, community, and trust can soften the raw edges of grief. It's about rebuilding connections to those around you and reconnecting with your own sense of worth and wholeness. The healing journey requires vulnerability, and through building authentic, supportive bonds, you can transform the isolation of grief into a shared experience that brings solace and support. Reconnecting with others—and with your own heart—will become a source of strength as you continue forward.

Making Sense Of It
The Transformative Power of Connection

Grief after abortion can create a subtle, almost invisible isolation. Even when surrounded by loved ones, it's possible to feel profoundly alone—because few have experienced this particular loss, and social stigma often silences conversation. Yet humans are wired for connection; our nervous systems thrive on safety, attunement, and empathy. When grief is carried in isolation, it can intensify, creating loops of shame, guilt, and self-blame. Connection, by contrast, interrupts these loops and offers a stabilizing, restorative force.

Psychologically, shared experience validates emotion. When someone acknowledges your grief without judgment—whether it's a partner, friend, support group, or therapist—it communicates, on a deeply neurological level, that your feelings are real, safe, and worthy of attention. The limbic system responds to this attunement by releasing oxytocin and reducing cortisol, fostering a sense of calm and safety in the body. Connection, then, is not just comfort—it is healing at the level of both mind and body.

From a sociological perspective, grief is deeply influenced by social narratives. Abortion, in particular, carries layers of cultural stigma that often tell people their feelings are invalid, fleeting, or wrong. By seeking or cultivating connection with those who affirm your experience, you push back against these cultural pressures and reclaim your narrative.

Making Sense Of It
The Transformative Power of Connection

Community can be small—one trusted friend, a peer support group, or even an online circle—but it matters because it allows you to witness and be witnessed, which is profoundly validating.

Healing through connection is also an internal process. Self-compassion functions as an internalized "safe other," allowing you to offer to yourself what you may not yet feel able to receive externally. Mindful practices, journaling letters to yourself, or speaking aloud your feelings are ways to build this internal attunement. Over time, internal and external connections reinforce each other, creating a feedback loop of safety, acknowledgment, and resilience.

Ultimately, embracing connection—both outward and inward—is an act of courage. It requires vulnerability, a willingness to be seen in your grief, and trust that your emotions will not break you. This openness transforms the isolating weight of sorrow into a shared human experience. Connection doesn't erase the pain, but it softens its edges, grounds you in safety, and reminds you that even in grief, you are not alone.

How have I been holding myself back from connecting with others?

After your abortion, you might have distanced yourself from others, either out of shame or because of the emotional weight you carry. Reflect on how you've been holding yourself back from connection, and why. How might opening up to someone in your life allow you to feel heard and supported? Write about the barriers you've built and what it might look like to gently begin breaking them down.

How have I been holding myself back from connecting with others?

Who in my life feels safe to talk to about my grief?

Not everyone in our lives may be equipped to hold space for our grief, and that's okay. But there are likely people who can provide the empathy, care, and understanding you need. Reflect on who in your circle feels like a safe person to share with. What qualities do they have that make them trustworthy? Write about the people you feel could help you carry your grief with compassion.

Who in my life feels safe to talk to about my grief?

What would it mean to truly listen to my inner voice with compassion?

Connecting with yourself can be just as important as connecting with others. This question encourages you to reflect on how you speak to yourself during grief. What is your internal dialogue like? Is it critical or compassionate? Write about what it would mean to change that voice to one that listens and nurtures, rather than judges or criticizes.

What would it mean to truly listen to my inner voice with compassion?

In what ways can I offer compassion to myself as I would to a close friend?

Often, we are our harshest critics, but when we turn that lens of compassion toward ourselves, healing can begin. Reflect on the ways you'd offer kindness and understanding to a loved one in grief. What would you say to them? Now, write down how you can offer that same compassion to yourself during this time of healing.

In what ways can I offer compassion to myself as I would to a close friend?

What do I need from others in my healing journey?

We all need different things in our healing process—some need space, others need company, some need advice, while others need silence. Reflect on what you specifically need from those around you during this time. Write about what support you need—whether it's emotional support, physical help, or someone to just listen without judgment.

What do I need from others in my healing journey?

TRACING THE TRUTH

SELF-COMPASSION LETTER

Sometimes the most powerful connection is the one we cultivate with ourselves. This exercise invites you to witness your own grief with kindness, building an internal "safe other."

Why it helps:
Writing a self-compassion letter strengthens internal attunement, offering validation and safety when external support may be limited. It reinforces the neurological and emotional pathways of connection, teaching your mind and body that grief can be held safely—both by yourself and others.

Begin by addressing yourself kindly: "Dear Me, I see you…"
Acknowledge the pain and complexity of your emotions: sadness, guilt, confusion, relief, or any other feeling. Let your words reflect understanding rather than judgment.
Offer reassurance and validation: "It's okay to feel this way. Your grief is real, and your experience matters."
Close with a gentle reminder of your strength and worth: "I am here for you. You are not alone. You are allowed to heal at your own pace."

TRACING THE TRUTH

SELF-COMPASSION LETTER

TRACING THE TRUTH

SELF-COMPASSION LETTER

TRACING THE TRUTH

SELF-COMPASSION LETTER

TRACING THE TRUTH

SELF-COMPASSION LETTER

TRACING THE TRUTH

MAPPING YOUR SUPPORT NETWORK

Connection heals, but it can feel invisible when grief isolates you. This exercise helps you identify and strengthen your sources of support—both human and internal—so you can actively nurture connection.

Why it helps:
Visualizing your support network reinforces the reality that you are not alone. It externalizes internal isolation, highlights existing resources, and empowers you to actively seek or strengthen connections that foster healing.

Draw a circle in the center of a page and label it "Me."
Around this circle, create smaller circles for people, communities, or practices that make you feel safe, seen, or supported. Include anyone you trust—a friend, partner, therapist, support group, or even an online community. Also include self-support practices, like journaling, meditation, or mindful breathing.
Draw lines connecting you to each circle and note what makes that connection supportive (e.g., "She listens without judgment," "Journaling helps me process emotions safely").

Reflect: Which connections feel strong? Which could use more attention? Are there ways you could cultivate new supportive ties?

TRACING THE TRUTH

MAPPING YOUR SUPPORT NETWORK

TRACING THE TRUTH

MAPPING YOUR SUPPORT NETWORK

TRACING THE TRUTH

MAPPING YOUR SUPPORT NETWORK

ACTION

CONNECTION FIRST

Relationships often fray not just from big conflicts, but from how we handle the everyday hard moments. GIVE is a simple skill to help you stay connected, even when the conversation is tough. It's about protecting the relationship while still being real. You don't have to agree with someone to treat them with respect—and sometimes, that tone alone changes the entire direction of the exchange.

Gentle

No attacks, threats, or judgments. Use a softer start. ("I know this is hard to talk about...")

Interested

Really listen. Nod, make space, ask small clarifying questions.

Validate

Acknowledge what makes sense in their perspective, even if you don't agree. ("I see why that would feel stressful for you.")

Easy manner

Keep a lightness. Humor if it feels right, relaxed body language, calm tone.

ACTION

HOLDING GROUND

Sometimes, the hardest part of communication isn't the other person—it's holding onto your own self-respect while you speak. FAST is about walking away from a conversation with your dignity intact, even if the other person didn't respond how you hoped. It's not about winning or being perfect—it's about staying fair, grounded, and aligned with who you want to be.

Fair

Be fair to both yourself and the other person. Avoid exaggerations or attacks.

(no) Apologies for existing

Don't over-apologize for having needs, feelings, or limits. Save "sorry" for true mistakes, not for breathing.

Stick to values

Stay anchored in what matters to you (kindness, honesty, respect, boundaries).

Truthful

No lies, excuses, or half-truths. Your integrity is your strength.

SECTION EIGHT

Forgiveness—Releasing the Burden of Guilt

Guilt often emerges after abortion. The conflicting emotions of choice and consequence can create an overwhelming sense of responsibility, as though you are carrying an invisible weight. Perhaps you feel like you made a decision that can never be undone, or you might question your choices with a harsh inner critic. These feelings can be isolating, and the weight of guilt can feel like a burden that never quite lifts.

But forgiveness—especially self-forgiveness—is a pathway to healing. It's the process of releasing the hold that guilt and self-blame have on your heart, allowing you to move forward with compassion for yourself. This section will guide you through the concept of forgiveness—not as a quick fix, but as a necessary, gradual, and deeply emotional process. We will explore how self-forgiveness begins with compassion and acceptance, giving you the emotional freedom to heal without the heavy burden of guilt.

Making Sense Of It
The Radical Act of Self-Forgiveness

Guilt after abortion is not just an emotion—it's a narrative that your mind repeats, a story that can loop endlessly, questioning your worth, your choices, and even your capacity to love yourself. Psychologically, guilt often arises from a mismatch between your values, your decisions, and the cultural or social expectations imposed on you. Even when you acted from necessity, safety, or clarity, the brain can magnify perceived "failures," creating an internalized judgment that feels heavier than any external critique.

Forgiveness is not about erasing memory or pretending the weight never existed. It is about acknowledging the complexity of your experience, validating the pain and conflicting emotions, and intentionally loosening the grip of self-blame. Neuroscience shows that self-directed compassion—an essential precursor to forgiveness—activates neural pathways that reduce stress responses in the amygdala while strengthening the prefrontal cortex's ability to regulate emotion. In simpler terms, practicing self-forgiveness rewires your brain to feel safer in your own body and less overwhelmed by persistent guilt.

From a sociological perspective, abortion grief occurs in a web of social silence and stigma. Guilt is often amplified by unspoken rules: the judgment of others, the culture of secrecy, the expectation that your grief should be hidden or minimized. By choosing self-forgiveness, you are actively countering these external pressures and reclaiming authority over your own emotional narrative. This is a radical act of autonomy—you are saying, "I will not let others' shame define my worth."

Making Sense Of It
The Radical Act of Self-Forgiveness

Forgiveness is also deeply relational, not just intrapersonal. The capacity to forgive yourself strengthens your ability to navigate interactions with others—partners, family, or friends—without allowing external judgment to compound internalized guilt. It creates a ripple effect: the more you offer compassion to yourself, the more you can accept empathy from others, and the more resilient you become in processing grief.

Ultimately, self-forgiveness is a practice, not a destination. It is the gradual loosening of guilt's hold, moment by moment, breath by breath. It is an ongoing conversation with yourself: I am human. I acted with intention. I deserve compassion. By embracing this practice, you release the weight of invisible burdens, making room for healing, clarity, and the freedom to move forward while honoring the fullness of your experience.

What does forgiveness mean to me?

Many of us carry ideas about forgiveness based on societal or familial expectations, but it's important to define it for yourself. Take some time to reflect on what forgiveness means to you, and how it might feel to truly forgive yourself for the decision you made. Is it about understanding? Compassion? Release? Write about what forgiveness would look like in your healing process.

What does forgiveness mean to me?

What beliefs about myself are tied to my guilt?

Guilt often stems from beliefs we hold about our character—about who we are as a person. Do you feel that you are "bad," "wrong," or "unworthy" because of your abortion? Reflect on how these beliefs influence your grief. Write about the ways in which guilt has shaped your self-image, and challenge these beliefs. Are they grounded in truth or in emotions that need healing?

What beliefs about myself are tied to my guilt?

How can I separate my decision from my self-worth?

It's easy to confuse a decision with our inherent worth as a person. You may feel like the decision you made defines you in a way that diminishes your value. Reflect on how you can separate your actions from your worth. Write about how you are more than any single decision you've made and how you deserve to treat yourself with kindness and compassion, regardless of your choices.

How can I separate my decision from my self-worth?

What would it look like to offer myself the same forgiveness I would offer a loved one?

Imagine a close friend who has made a similar choice and is carrying guilt. What would you say to them? How would you comfort and support them? Write about how you can extend the same compassion to yourself. Reflect on what it would feel like to offer yourself the same forgiveness that you would so freely offer others.

What would it look like to offer myself the same forgiveness I would offer a loved one?

How can I begin to let go of guilt, one step at a time?

Forgiveness is a gradual process. It doesn't happen overnight. What small, compassionate steps can you take to begin releasing the guilt that weighs on you? Write about one step you can take today to lighten this burden—whether it's through a self-compassionate affirmation, a conversation with a trusted friend, or a deep breath to acknowledge that you are worthy of healing.

How can I begin to let go of guilt, one step at a time?

ACTION

REALITY CHECK QUESTIONS

Life throws challenges at us constantly—decisions, conflicts, or situations that leave us feeling stuck. When our minds spin in worry or frustration, it's hard to see a way out. A problem-solving worksheet helps you slow down and approach the situation with clarity. By defining the problem, brainstorming options without judgment, choosing a practical path, and planning small steps, you gain control over what you can influence. Reviewing outcomes afterwards teaches you what works and what needs adjustment, helping you navigate challenges more confidently.

Think of one situation that's been weighing on you or leaving you stuck—big or small—and write it down in one sentence

- 01 Define the problem in one sentence.
- 02 Brainstorm options
- 03 Pick a "good-enough" option.
- 04 Plan the steps
- 05 Review results and tweak.

ACTION

RESILIENCE LOG

When life feels heavy, it's easy to overlook all the ways you're managing, showing up, or making a difference—especially when old beliefs tell you you're not enough. This log helps you notice the small but real evidence of your resilience, care, and competence each day. Recording these moments rewires your focus from what went wrong to what actually happened, giving your mind proof that you are capable, contributing, and connected. Ending with a short reflection ties it all together, reinforcing a more balanced and compassionate view of yourself.

Record daily moments where you are:

Coping with a challenge (e.g., managing a tense conversation, taking a pause before reacting).
Contributing or helping (e.g., supporting a friend, completing a task, showing up for someone).
Connecting (e.g., reaching out to someone, expressing your feelings, listening fully).

End each entry with a reflection:
"What this says about me is ___." Example: "I am capable of handling difficult moments with care."

Review weekly. Notice patterns of strength, resilience, and connection that you might normally overlook.

Day	Coping with a challenge	Contributing or helping	Connecting	Reflection

ACTION

RESILIENCE LOG

Day	Coping with a challenge	Contributing or helping	Connecting	Reflection

SECTION NINE

Reclaiming Your Power—Embracing the Path Forward

The pain of loss can feel like it erases parts of you—your sense of self, your sense of power, your belief in what you can still achieve. You might feel disconnected from the person you were before the abortion, unsure of how to rebuild after such a profound emotional experience. It can be difficult to imagine how you can move forward or what your future looks like when your heart feels shattered by grief.

But the truth is, you are not broken. You are not defined by any single experience, no matter how painful or complex. Your inner strength—your ability to heal, to grow, to rise again—is far greater than you may realize. This section is here to help you reconnect with that power and to envision a future where healing is possible and self-empowerment is within reach. You deserve to feel whole again, to trust yourself again, and to live a life that reflects the strength and resilience you carry within you.

Making Sense Of It
Rediscovering Strength After Loss

Experiencing grief after an abortion can create a profound sense of disconnection—not only from your body and emotions but also from your own agency. When the mind and heart are preoccupied with loss, regret, or societal judgment, it's easy to feel as though the ability to make decisions, to trust yourself, or to envision a meaningful future has been stripped away. Psychologically, this is natural: intense grief often hijacks executive functioning, narrows focus to survival and emotion regulation, and can leave the prefrontal cortex—the part of the brain responsible for planning, self-reflection, and self-efficacy—overwhelmed. The result is a temporary erosion of confidence and a sense of powerlessness.

Reclaiming your power begins with recognizing that power is not something lost—it is always present, lying dormant under layers of guilt, shame, and emotional turbulence. Cognitive neuroscience shows that intentional reflection and action can reactivate neural pathways associated with agency and resilience. When you begin to set small, meaningful goals, make conscious choices for yourself, or engage in acts that honor your values, your brain starts to reinforce the experience of competence and self-efficacy. Each small act of reclaiming choice rewires the internal narrative: I can act. I can decide. I am capable.

From a sociocultural perspective, reproductive decisions are often judged or scrutinized, which can amplify internalized shame and diminish perceived autonomy.

Making Sense Of It
Rediscovering Strength After Loss

Recognizing that your decision was made in alignment with your needs, values, and circumstances is a profound act of self-validation. By intentionally reconnecting with your own narrative, you counteract external pressures, reclaim authorship of your life story, and affirm your right to define what "moving forward" looks like.

Reclaiming power also requires integrating mind and body. Somatic experiences—feeling your breath, noticing bodily sensations, and engaging in movements that convey strength—help anchor psychological resilience in tangible, physical ways. Trauma-informed research suggests that somatic reconnection reinforces the nervous system's sense of safety and agency, allowing grief to coexist with empowerment rather than being a suppressive force.

Ultimately, reclaiming your power is a layered, ongoing process. It is both internal and external, cognitive and somatic, subtle and profound. It is a conscious decision to honor your strength, to trust your judgment, and to envision a future shaped by your values rather than your fears. Even after the most challenging experiences, the capacity to heal, to rebuild, and to thrive remains within you—waiting for recognition, cultivation, and affirmation.

What does personal power look like to me now?

Take a moment to reflect on how you define personal power. What does it look like for you after grief? Is it about reclaiming your choices? Is it about rediscovering your voice or your purpose? Write about what power means to you today, and how it might have changed over the course of your journey.

What does personal power look like to me now?

What strengths have I discovered in myself through this process?

Even in the most painful experiences, we can uncover strengths we didn't know we had. Reflect on the qualities you've noticed in yourself since the abortion—whether it's resilience, courage, self-awareness, or the ability to face difficult emotions. Write about the strengths you've discovered and how they've shaped your journey.

What strengths have I discovered in myself through this process?

How do I envision my future now, and how can I start to shape it?

It may be difficult to see beyond your grief, but try to imagine a future where you have healed and grown. What do you want your life to look like in 6 months, 1 year, or 5 years? Write about the goals, dreams, and aspirations you still hold, and reflect on the steps you can take—however small—towards them. How can you start shaping your future today?

How do I envision my future now, and how can I start to shape it?

What would it mean to live without regret or shame?

Regret and shame are often intertwined with the grief of abortion. But what if, instead of living with these heavy emotions, you allowed yourself to release them? How would it feel to live without carrying that weight? Write about what it would be like to live without regret or shame, and how that might free you to fully embrace your future.

What would it mean to live without regret or shame?

What steps can I take today to reclaim my life and my sense of self?

Empowerment begins with action, even if it's small. What is one step you can take today to reconnect with yourself, your values, or your passions? Write about what feels right for you—whether it's setting a boundary, engaging in a hobby, or simply practicing self-care. Every small action contributes to reclaiming your power.

What steps can I take today to reclaim my life and my sense of self?

TRACING THE TRUTH

POWER TIMELINE

When grief follows a deeply personal choice, it can feel like your agency has been taken. This exercise helps you track moments of personal power throughout your life, reminding you that your capacity to act and decide has always been within you—even if it feels buried now.

Why it helps:
Seeing your history of agency visually reminds you that power is not lost—it has always been part of your story. It strengthens self-efficacy and builds confidence in your ability to make empowered choices moving forward.

Draw a horizontal line across a page. Label the left end "Past" and the right end "Future."
Mark significant moments in your life along the line where you exercised personal strength, made a choice that aligned with your values, or overcame a challenge—no matter how small. Include the recent decision around your abortion.
Under each point, write a brief note about the strength or resource you drew on.

Reflect: How have these moments shaped your ability to reclaim power now? How can you carry this strength into the next steps of your life?

TRACING THE TRUTH

POWER TIMELINE

TRACING THE TRUTH

FUTURE SELF VISION

Reclaiming power includes imagining a future where you feel capable, resilient, and whole. This exercise guides you to articulate that vision and connect emotionally with the empowered version of yourself.

Why it helps:
Envisioning your empowered future activates your brain's planning and motivation centers, strengthening belief in self-efficacy. It creates a bridge between current grief and the capacity for resilience, helping you reconnect with your inner authority and agency.

Close your eyes and imagine yourself one year from now, having reclaimed your strength after this period of grief. What does your life look like? How do you carry yourself? How do you respond to challenges?
Open your eyes and write a letter to your future self, describing the qualities you want to embody, the choices you hope to make, and the ways you will honor your own agency.
Include affirmations like: "I trust myself," "I am capable," "I am allowed to rebuild on my own terms."
Revisit this letter whenever you feel disconnected from your power or unsure of your next steps.

TRACING THE TRUTH

FUTURE SELF VISION

TRACING THE TRUTH

FUTURE SELF VISION

TRACING THE TRUTH

FUTURE SELF VISION

TRACING THE TRUTH

FUTURE SELF VISION

ACTION

THE TRIGGER MAP

When you react automatically, it often feels like there's no pause between what happens and how you respond. This exercise helps you slow things down and see the chain of events clearly—what triggered the feeling, the thought that popped up, the urge, and what actually happened. Once you can see it all laid out, you can spot the point where you can intervene next time. That small pause is enough to change the outcome, give yourself more control, and break patterns that have been running on autopilot.

Map the chain: Write down each step in order

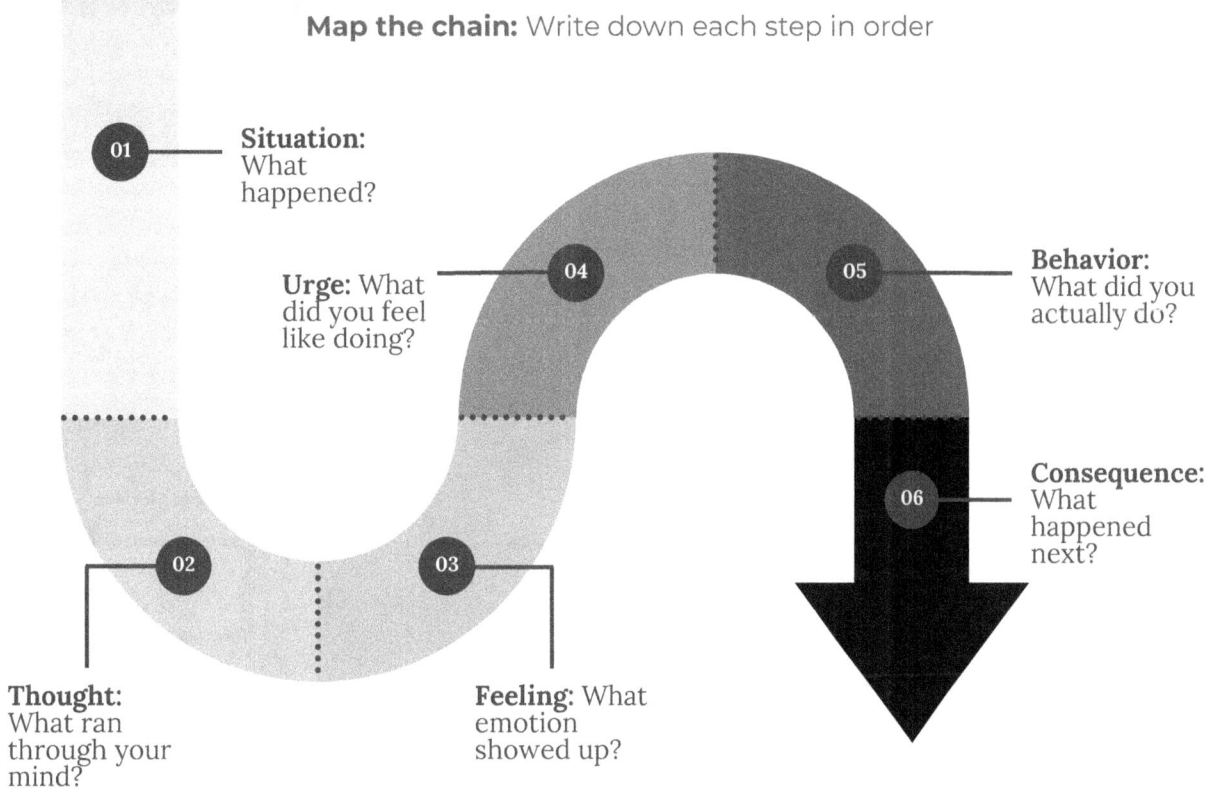

01 **Situation:** What happened?

02 **Thought:** What ran through your mind?

03 **Feeling:** What emotion showed up?

04 **Urge:** What did you feel like doing?

05 **Behavior:** What did you actually do?

06 **Consequence:** What happened next?

Circle your change point. Look at the chain and find the first step where you could intervene next time.

Plan one interruption. Pick a tool or skill to use—like a short breathing exercise, a script you can say, or a grounding move—to pause the chain and respond differently.

ACTION

CLIMBING DOWN

When your mind hits you with a brutal thought—like "I always mess up"—it can feel impossible to jump straight to a positive or kind belief. Your brain just won't buy it. This exercise gives you a middle ground. By writing the harsh thought at the top and gradually stepping down to gentler, more realistic versions, you give yourself space to find a statement that actually feels believable. Even if it's not perfect, that 70% believable thought is enough to lower the intensity and guide you toward calmer choices today.

Write the harsh thought at the top rung. (e.g., "I always mess up.")
Step down slowly. Each rung is a slightly softer, more balanced version of the thought.
  "I mess up sometimes, but not always."
  "Everyone makes mistakes. Mine don't erase the things I do well."
  "I can learn from this and try again."
Pick the rung that feels about 70% true. You don't have to land at the bottom. Just stop where it feels believable.
Act from that rung. Let today's choices come from this steadier, more grounded statement.

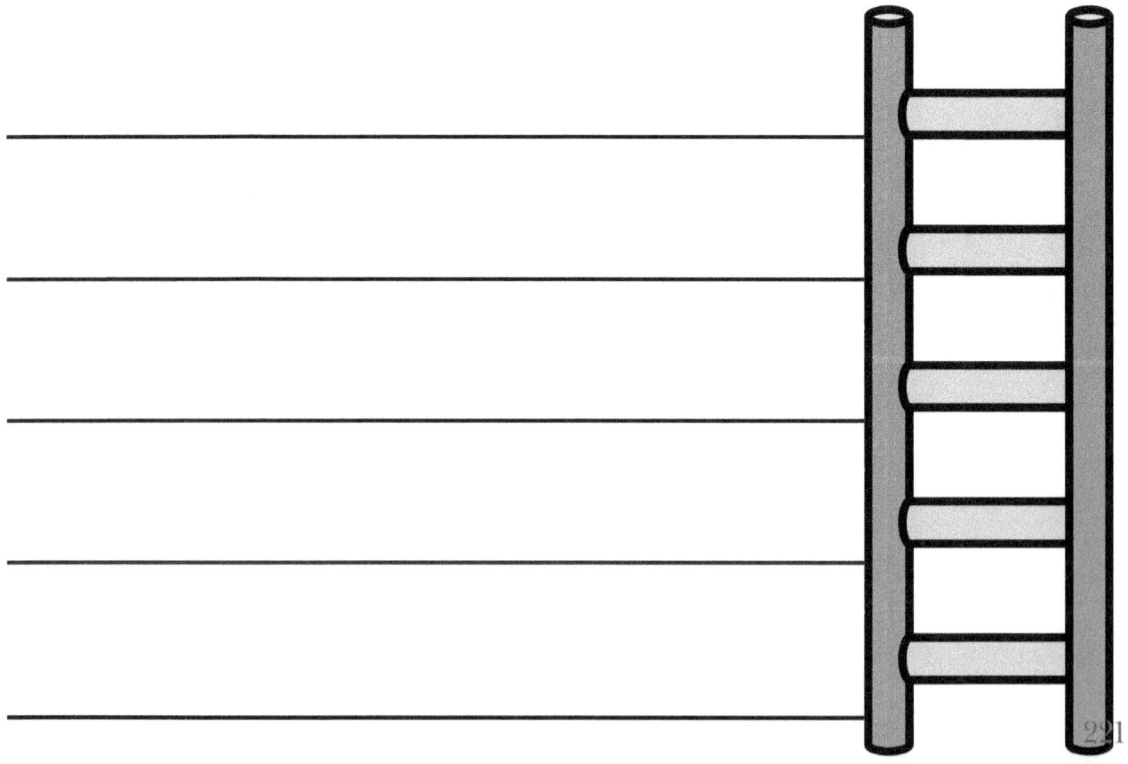

SECTION TEN

Embracing Peace – Living With Yourself After the Journey

It's one of the deepest, most confusing emotional wounds: when the people who are supposed to "become family" instead become a source of chronic pain, disrespect, or fear. You may have tried everything — being kind, keeping the peace, setting boundaries, explaining yourself — and still found yourself walking on eggshells or questioning your own sanity. Maybe others don't see it. Maybe your partner doesn't fully get it. Maybe you've even wondered if you are the problem. You're not.

This kind of relational harm often goes unrecognized — but it's real. And it's traumatic. It erodes your sense of safety, dignity, and belonging, especially when it happens inside a family system you're supposed to merge with. Whether the damage is overt or subtle, loud or quiet, intentional or unconscious, it matters because it hurts you. And here, finally, is a space where that pain will be named, held, and healed — without minimizing, gaslighting, or guilt.

Making Sense Of It
Coexisting with Grief as a Path to Peace

After grief, especially the complex grief that follows abortion, the mind often clings to a sense of incompleteness—a belief that peace is only possible once pain has vanished. But psychologically, peace is not a state of absence; it is a state of coexistence. Research on grief and trauma consistently shows that attempts to "erase" emotional pain or rush toward closure can backfire, intensifying guilt, shame, or avoidance. True healing, rather, comes from learning to integrate the full spectrum of your experience—the sorrow, the relief, the regret, and the resilience—into a coherent narrative of self.

Neuroscience provides insight into why this works. When we acknowledge and name emotions rather than suppress them, the brain's limbic system (which governs emotional processing) can gradually communicate with the prefrontal cortex (which governs reasoning and perspective). This communication allows difficult feelings to exist without overwhelming the system, creating space for emotional regulation and reflective insight. In simpler terms, the brain learns that grief and joy can coexist—that one does not cancel the other.

From a social perspective, grief after abortion is often invisible. Many people experience what is called "disenfranchised grief," where societal norms minimize or invalidate the loss. Living with this kind of grief requires cultivating internal validation—learning to honor your own experience even when it is unacknowledged by others.

Making Sense Of It
Coexisting with Grief as a Path to Peace

This internal affirmation is a critical component of emotional resilience, helping you to hold both grief and hope in your mind simultaneously.

Anthropologically, rites of passage, mourning rituals, and symbolic acts across cultures reflect the human need to process loss without erasing it. Embracing peace after abortion similarly involves creating personal rituals—internal or external—that allow you to recognize the significance of your journey while continuing to live fully.

Ultimately, embracing peace is an act of self-compassion and cognitive integration. It is choosing to sit alongside your pain without letting it define you, creating a sense of continuity between who you were, who you are, and who you are becoming. Peace is not a finish line; it is the ongoing capacity to engage with life fully, with awareness, acceptance, and a gentle acknowledgment that you have survived, learned, and grown.

What does peace look like for me, right now?

Peace may not look like what you expected, and that's okay. Take a moment to reflect on what peace actually feels like for you, in this season of your life. What would it mean to have peace, even if your grief isn't fully gone? Write about what peace looks like and feels like for you right now.

What does peace look like for me, right now?

What does self-forgiveness mean to me, and how can I begin to practice it?

Forgiveness doesn't happen overnight, but it's a necessary step in finding peace. What does it mean to forgive yourself for the grief, the decisions, and the struggles you've experienced? Write about what self-forgiveness might look like in your life, and what small steps you can take to begin this process.

What does self-forgiveness mean to me, and how can I begin to practice it?

What small practices can I integrate into my daily routine to help me find peace?

Peace often comes through small, intentional practices—whether it's journaling, deep breathing, or taking a walk. What are some small practices you can incorporate into your day that will help you feel more grounded, peaceful, and present? Write about these practices and how they might support your emotional healing.

What small practices can I integrate into my daily routine to help me find peace?

What am I grateful for today, even in the midst of my grief?

Grief often makes it difficult to see the good, but there are always things to be grateful for. Take a moment to write about what you're grateful for today. It could be a person, an experience, or simply the fact that you are alive and continuing to heal. Gratitude can help shift our focus from what is lost to what is still here.

What am I grateful for today, even in the midst of my grief?

How can I integrate my grief into my life without letting it define me?

Grief will always be a part of you, but it doesn't have to be your defining feature. How can you honor your grief while still living fully? Write about how you can create space for your grief without letting it take over your identity. How can you hold both the pain and the peace in your life at the same time?

How can I integrate my grief into my life without letting it define me?

ACTION

COOL & RESET

Our nervous system reacts to temperature in ways that can quickly shift arousal. Cool sensations on the face or neck signal the body that danger is passing, helping to calm adrenaline and stress. Spending just a minute noticing the change gives your mind a break from racing thoughts and brings your body into a calmer state — a small but powerful way to regain presence and control.

Find a safe source of cool — a cold pack, splash of water, or even holding something cool in your hands.

Bring it gently to your face or neck. Focus on the sensation for about 60 seconds.

Notice the temperature, the pressure, the way your skin responds, and let your breathing follow the rhythm of the sensation.

ACTION

SEEING THE BIGGER PICTURE

When someone's behavior triggers you—or when you catch yourself blaming yourself—your mind often jumps to the harshest story: "It's all my fault," or "They're deliberately hurting me." Compassionate Reattribution helps you pause and look at the situation more realistically. By considering context, other explanations, and human limits, you can soften blame, see things more fairly, and plan a small step to repair or respond thoughtfully. It doesn't excuse harmful behavior, but it frees your mind from spinning in harsh judgments.

Identify the blamey thought.
Example: "I shouldn't have said that—now they're upset."

Consider other explanations.
Context: maybe they had a rough day.
Skills: maybe they struggle to communicate.
Nervous system: stress can make anyone react sharply.

Choose a fair attribution.
Example: "They were stressed, not necessarily upset at me personally."

Pick one small repair step (if needed).
Example: check in calmly, clarify your intent, or take a pause before responding.

BLAMEY THOUGHT	OTHER EXPLANATIONS	FAIR ATTRIBUTION & REPAIR STEP

ACTION

SEEING THE BIGGER PICTURE

BLAMEY THOUGHT	OTHER EXPLANATIONS	FAIR ATTRIBUTION & REPAIR STEP

SECTION ELEVEN

The Future, Reimagined – Navigating the Emotions of Future Pregnancies

The idea of pregnancy after abortion can stir up a complex mix of emotions. On one hand, there may be fear and uncertainty, or even guilt about wanting to try again. On the other hand, there may also be hope—hope that the future can offer something different, something healing. For many, this is a deeply personal and sometimes unsettling part of their healing journey. There's no right or wrong way to feel about the possibility of future pregnancies, and there's no timeline for when or how you should be "ready" for such an experience.

This section is about giving space to those feelings—the fears, the hopes, the hesitations—and supporting you in navigating the emotional terrain of pregnancy as a possibility in the future. Whether you want to become pregnant again or whether you feel unsure about what that might look like, this section is about helping you feel safe with your emotions, whatever they may be. It's about allowing yourself to grow into whatever your future holds, free from pressure or shame. Healing doesn't mean you need to make decisions right away, but it does mean you're free to explore your emotional landscape in a way that is gentle, kind, and empowering.

Making Sense Of It
Embracing Uncertainty and Complexity in Future Fertility

The prospect of future pregnancies after abortion often evokes a paradoxical mix of hope and fear—a duality that is completely natural but can feel destabilizing. Psychologically, this reflects what researchers describe as "ambiguous future-oriented grief": a recognition of potential joy, alongside the lingering shadow of past loss. Our brains are wired to anticipate risk and reward, which means it's common to feel both protective caution and eager curiosity at the same time. This tension is not a sign of weakness; it is evidence that your emotional system is working to safeguard both your heart and your choices.

Cognitively, navigating these emotions requires building what psychologists call "tolerances for uncertainty." This is the capacity to sit with the unknown without rushing to resolve it or judge yourself for feeling conflicted. By naming your feelings—fear, excitement, hesitation, hope—you activate your prefrontal cortex, which helps regulate the limbic system and allows for more conscious, reflective decision-making. In practice, this can mean acknowledging your nervousness about trying again while simultaneously noticing moments of curiosity or cautious optimism.

Socially and culturally, the topic of pregnancy after abortion is heavily loaded. Disenfranchised grief and societal expectations often amplify self-judgment: "Am I ready? Will others approve? Is it selfish to hope?" These internalized pressures can create a feedback loop of guilt, anxiety, and overthinking.

Making Sense Of It
Embracing Uncertainty and Complexity in Future Fertility

Recognizing these pressures as external influences—rather than inherent truths—allows you to reclaim your autonomy and approach future decisions from a grounded, self-directed place.

Anthropologically, humans have long used rituals, narratives, and storytelling to prepare for life's uncertainties. You can create your own symbolic practices—quiet reflection, journaling, or visualizations—to honor both the lessons of the past and the possibilities of the future. By integrating your grief and hope, you allow your emotional system to carry both without being paralyzed by either.

Ultimately, navigating future pregnancies after abortion is less about certainty and more about agency. It is about cultivating a compassionate inner dialogue, recognizing the validity of every emotion, and allowing yourself to move forward at your own pace. Healing doesn't require immediate action; it requires presence, self-compassion, and the courage to envision what may come—holding hope and caution side by side as part of a resilient, empowered emotional life.

What fears or anxieties do I have about getting pregnant again in the future?

Acknowledge the fears you might hold about future pregnancies. Are you afraid of losing control? Of repeating a past experience? Of judgment from others? Writing down these fears will help you see them for what they are—emotions that are valid but don't need to define your future. Take a moment to gently examine what's underneath your fears. Are they tied to your past grief? Are they about the unknowns of the future? Allow yourself the space to process these anxieties without judgment.

What fears or anxieties do I have about getting pregnant again in the future?

What would I need to feel emotionally ready for a future pregnancy?

If you're considering the possibility of becoming pregnant again, what emotional conditions would need to be in place for you to feel safe and prepared? Would you need more time to heal emotionally? More support from loved ones? Professional therapy or healing practices? Write about what would make you feel emotionally grounded and capable of navigating a future pregnancy. This is a process that requires self-compassion, and it's important to recognize what you might need in order to feel ready.

What would I need to feel emotionally ready for a future pregnancy?

How do I see myself moving forward with pregnancy?

Whether you want to get pregnant again or you feel unsure, this question is about your vision for your future self. Take a moment to reflect on how you see yourself moving forward. Are there fears, hopes, or desires tied to this vision? How does your emotional healing shape the way you imagine pregnancy? This journal prompt is designed to help you explore what you envision, giving you the freedom to change your mind, and honoring that you have choices.

How do I see myself moving forward with pregnancy?

What messages would I need to give myself in order to feel safe in the possibility of another pregnancy?

The messages we tell ourselves shape how we feel. What affirmations or reassuring words do you need to say to yourself to feel safe and at peace with the possibility of another pregnancy? These might be affirmations about your own strength, your ability to heal, or your right to make your own choices. Write down a few messages that you can remind yourself of if and when the time comes to make a decision about the future.

What messages would I need to give myself in order to feel safe in the possibility of another pregnancy?

How can I process the emotions of future pregnancies without feeling pressured or rushed?

It's common to feel pressure from society, from family, or even from yourself to "move on" or "get over it." But your healing journey has its own pace, and it's important to honor that. Take time to reflect on how you can create space for your emotions, without rushing or forcing a decision about future pregnancies. Write about the pressure you feel (if any), and how you can release that pressure in order to move forward at your own pace. This is about giving yourself permission to heal and make decisions when and how you're ready.

How can I process the emotions of future pregnancies without feeling pressured or rushed?

TRACING THE TRUTH

SETTING EMOTIONAL BOUNDARIES FOR THE FUTURE

Imagining a future pregnancy can bring up a mix of excitement, fear, and uncertainty. This exercise helps you clarify what you need emotionally to feel safe, supported, and empowered as you consider your options.

Why it helps:
This exercise transforms abstract worries into concrete actions. It strengthens your autonomy, teaches self-compassion, and creates a protective framework that allows you to hold both hope and caution without being overwhelmed. By proactively defining supports and limits, you create emotional space to explore future possibilities safely and intentionally.

Under Supports I Need, list people, practices, or internal resources that make you feel safe and validated—this could include a therapist, a trusted friend, journaling, or mindfulness exercises.

Under Boundaries I Want, list situations, conversations, or pressures you need to limit or avoid—anything that may provoke guilt, anxiety, or shame.

Reflect on how you can communicate these supports and boundaries to yourself and others. Consider small, practical steps to uphold them.

TRACING THE TRUTH

SETTING EMOTIONAL BOUNDARIES FOR THE FUTURE

Supports I Need　　　　　　　　　　**Boundaries I Want**

TRACING THE TRUTH

FUTURE LANDSCAPE

Sometimes, your feelings about future pregnancies can be confusing or even contradictory. This exercise helps you name and visualize your emotions so you can approach them with clarity and compassion.

Why it helps:
Mapping emotions makes the invisible visible. It allows you to acknowledge both hope and fear without judgment, helping your brain integrate complex feelings rather than suppressing them. It also fosters self-compassion and awareness, crucial for making empowered future decisions.

Draw a large circle on a page, divided into four quadrants.
Label the quadrants: Hope, Fear, Excitement, Hesitation.
Fill in each quadrant with words, phrases, or images that represent your current feelings about the possibility of future pregnancy. Include both subtle and intense emotions.

Reflect on the overlaps or contradictions. Which feelings are strongest? Which are quiet but persistent?

TRACING THE TRUTH

FUTURE LANDSCAPE

ACTION

MOMENTS OF LIGHT

When life feels heavy, it's easy to overlook the small, positive moments that actually keep us grounded. Intentionally creating and noticing positive experiences rewires your brain to notice what feels good, rather than only what feels wrong. Over time, these moments build momentum, helping you feel more resilient, connected, and capable. Short-term enjoyment strengthens your nervous system's sense of safety; long-term, value-aligned actions help you create a life that genuinely feels worth living.

Schedule small joys daily

Pick one tiny thing each day that sparks a little happiness—coffee in silence, a walk, listening to music, a funny video.

Record the experience

Write down how it felt in the moment.

Plan one value-aligned action per week

Something bigger that aligns with your goals or values—reaching out to a friend, pursuing a hobby, volunteering.

Reflect on impact

Notice shifts in mood, energy, or perspective after small and larger actions.

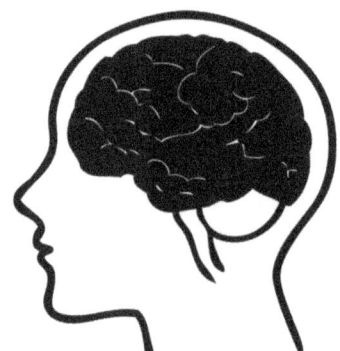

Repeat consistently

Gradually, these small and larger positive moments accumulate to create lasting emotional lift.

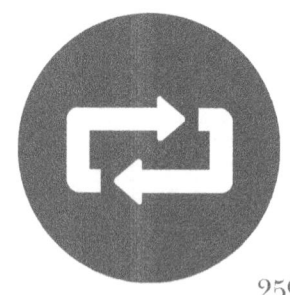

STONEWELL HEALING PRESS

ASSESSMENT

HOW FAR I'VE COME

You've done the work — now let's see where you're at. Take a moment to rate these statements again with honesty and self-compassion. Notice what's shifted, what still feels raw, and what that means for your next steps.

1-10

1   I feel able to acknowledge and honor all of my emotions—even the conflicting or uncomfortable ones—without self-judgment.

2   I feel genuine compassion and forgiveness toward myself for the choices I've made and the experiences I've lived.

3   I feel confident in my ability to make decisions that reflect my values, needs, and boundaries.

4   I feel clarity and understanding about the ways my past experiences impact my emotions and relationships today.

5   I feel capable of holding hope for the future while allowing myself to fully feel past grief and loss.

6   I feel supported and understood by people, communities, or practices that honor my experience.

7   I feel able to navigate conversations, social expectations, or judgments about my experience without losing my emotional center.

8   I feel empowered to reclaim my personal strength, autonomy, and agency in my healing journey and in life moving forward.

Mindset & Identity Shift Reflection

Healing changes the way you see yourself. You might notice you're less reactive in certain moments, more confident speaking up, or simply softer with yourself. This page is about spotting those shifts — the ones that show you're not the same person who started this journey.

In what ways do I see myself differently than when I started?

What beliefs about myself or others are shifting?

How has my sense of hope, strength, or trust evolved?

MOVING FORWARD

ACTION PLAN

This is your personalized roadmap for continuing growth beyond this workbook. Use this space to clarify which skills you'll keep practicing, how you'll notice early warning signs, and what concrete steps you'll take to support yourself. Remember, transformation happens one intentional step at a time.

Skills I will keep practicing regularly	
Early warning signs or triggers I'll watch for:	
When I notice these signs, here's what I will do:	

MOVING FORWARD

ACTION PLAN

This is your personalized roadmap for continuing growth beyond this workbook. Use this space to clarify which skills you'll keep practicing, how you'll notice early warning signs, and what concrete steps you'll take to support yourself. Remember, transformation happens one intentional step at a time.

Ways I can check in with myself to monitor progress (daily, weekly, monthly):

People or supports I will reach out to if I need encouragement or accountability:

One commitment I'm making to myself right now:

RESOURCE LIST

The resources listed here are shared for informational purposes only. While they provide valuable support and tools for mental health, I am not endorsing or guaranteeing the quality, effectiveness, or availability of their services. It's important to explore these options and verify the details directly on their websites to ensure they align with your personal needs.

National Alliance on Mental Illness ☐

www.nami.org

Offers free mental health education, peer support, and a 24/7 helpline.

Insight Timer ☐

www.insighttimer.com

A free meditation app with thousands of guided meditations, music, and talks on mental well-being

Planned Parenthood ☐

www.plannedparenthood.org/international

Offers resources, training, and advice on how parents can support their child's mental health, including guides and printable resources.

Crisis Text Line ☐

www.crisistextline.org

Offers free, 24/7 text-based support for mental health crises

7 Cups ☐

www.7cups.com

Offers free, anonymous online chat with trained volunteers, as well as paid therapy with licensed professionals.

Grief after abortion is something that's barely spoken about in the world, let alone in relationships. It's often this quiet, private thing—where even if you've opened up to a few people, you can't quite bring yourself to open up to yourself fully. It feels like there's a part of you, deep down, that's still holding back. The emotions are layered, complicated, and at times, they're just too hard to unravel alone. And that's okay. Because you're not supposed to go through this by yourself. There's so much complexity in abortion grief—grief for the choice, grief for the unknown, grief for what could've been. It's not something that fits neatly into the box of "regret" or "relief," and honestly, society doesn't make space for it. People don't always know what to say or how to be there, and even when they try, it's hard to truly open up. The world doesn't always feel safe enough to let these emotions spill out. But here's the thing: it's essential that you let yourself feel. Even if it's messy, even if it doesn't make sense, even if it's uncomfortable. You deserve to give yourself that permission. There's healing in the space where you can sit with your grief, no matter how complex or confusing it feels. There's power in being able to shuffle through those layers, one by one, and sort out the feelings that have been quietly living inside you.

So, if nothing else, remember this: you don't have to carry this alone. The journey of abortion grief can be isolating, but it doesn't have to be permanent. Opening up, even just to yourself, is one of the most profound ways you can heal.

M. Tourangeau
Stonewell Healing Press

www.ingramcontent.com/pod-product-compliance
Lightning Source LLC
Chambersburg PA
CBHW080836230426

43665CB00021B/2859